TALKING TO THE S   ＿PERS

Copyright © 2022 Sage Birchwater
01 02 03 04 05 26 25 24 23 22

All rights reserved. No part of this publication may be reproduced, stored in a retrieval system or transmitted, in any form or by any means, without prior permission of the publisher or, in the case of photocopying or other reprographic copying, a licence from Access Copyright, the Canadian Copyright Licensing Agency, www.accesscopyright.ca, 1-800-893-5777, info@access-copyright.ca.

Caitlin Press Inc.
3375 Ponderosa Way
Qualicum Beach, BC V9K 2J8
www.caitlin-press.com

Text and cover design by Vici Johnstone
Cover photo by Sage Birchwater
Edited by Meg Yamamoto

Printed in Canada

Caitlin Press Inc. acknowledges financial support from the Government of Canada and the Canada Council for the Arts, and the Province of British Columbia through the British Columbia Arts Council and the Book Publisher's Tax Credit.

Library and Archives Canada Cataloguing in Publication

Talking to the story keepers : tales from the Chilcotin Plateau / by Sage Birchwater.
Birchwater, Sage, author.
Canadiana 20210317159 | ISBN 9781773860800 (softcover)
LCSH: Indigenous peoples—British Columbia—Chilcotin Plateau. | LCSH: Indigenous peoples—
British Columbia—Chilcotin Plateau—History. | LCSH: Indigenous peoples—British Columbia—
Chilcotin Plateau—Biography. | LCSH: Chilcotin Plateau (B.C.)—History. | LCGFT: Biographies.

LCC E78.B9 B57 2022 | DDC 971.1/7500497—dc23

TALKING TO THE STORY KEEPERS

TALES FROM THE CHILCOTIN PLATEAU

SAGE BIRCHWATER

CAITLIN PRESS 2022

CONTENTS

Willie Sulin, the son of Tŝilhqot'in father Frank Sulin and Dakelh mother Ellie Stillas Sulin, was the second husband of Lucy Dagg Dester Sulin. Willie and Lucy made their home at Towdystan. Sage Birchwater photo

Introduction

I first heard about the Chilcotin when I was living in Toronto during the winter of 1972–73. An article in an underground newspaper told the sad details of the death of a Tŝilhqot'in man, Fred Quilt, at the hands of the RCMP. It was on a cold winter night near Alexis Creek, west of Williams Lake. The inquest into Fred's death made national headlines. What exactly happened was never clear. The police said one thing and the Tŝilhqot'in witnesses said something different.

But it was obvious there were deep-seated inequities in the Chilcotin that had to change. Chalk it up to systemic racism in which Tŝilhqot'in citizens were being marginalized in their own country. For more than a century, colonial settlers had been moving in and taking up land that had once been the exclusive domain of the Tŝilhqot'in Nation, and little could be done to stem the tide. The Canadian political and legal system was bent that way.

What was on trial besides the circumstances of Fred Quilt's death was the dirt-poor attitude mainstream society had toward the Tŝilhqot'in People. The incident became a trigger point questioning how Indigenous people were being treated across Canada.

The inquest drew big-city media to the small town of Williams Lake in the BC interior. The locals weren't used to such scrutiny of the status quo. The most attention the town usually mustered was during those few days in summer when the community hosted its annual stampede.

The inquest brought other stories to light. One in particular grabbed my attention. It told of a Tŝilhqot'in recluse, Chiwid, who lived outside year-round and withstood the harsh Chilcotin winter when temperatures regularly dropped to −50°C for weeks at a time. Her survival bespoke something deeper and more profound: that the Chilcotin itself was so wild and unfettered as to allow an individual like Chiwid the freedom to live her life as she chose.

So I was intrigued and made up my mind to head back home to British Columbia and check out the Cariboo Chilcotin Coast for myself. That was nearly fifty years ago, and the country remains a treasure trove of stories and adventure.

The early 1970s was the apex of the back-to-the-land movement. This was a phenomenon occurring worldwide but particularly in North America, where thousands of young people from middle-class families were seeking alternatives to the status quo. Many were drawn to the Cariboo Chilcotin Coast.

I was twenty-four when fate plunked me down in Williams Lake in April 1973. My closest neighbours were Dave and Nene Twan, who lived just down the alley from 280 North Mackenzie Avenue, where I lived with a group of friends. We occupied three small cabins at the corner of Cameron Street and North Mackenzie.

Dave Twan was a natural storyteller. He was born in 1906 at the old Fort Alexandria along the Fraser River between Williams Lake and Quesnel. His father, John Sanford Twan, had also been born there, in 1853, and John pre-empted the old fort in 1895 after the Hudson's Bay Company executed a quit claim on the property. Dave's mother, Rosalie Sam Hunt, was a Dakelh woman born next to the fort at ?Esdilagh.

It was probably Dave who taught me how stories could convey the essential history of a place. We visited his old stomping grounds at Alexandria several times, and his stories brought the landscape alive.

THUNDER BERT AND THE TROOPERS OF WILLIAMS LAKE

I spent four years in Williams Lake and gradually got to know the Indigenous street people known locally as the Troopers. Alcohol was a preoccupation for them. That's why they were in town. The liquor store was on First Avenue, just half a block up from my place, so a handy drinking spot to share a jug of wine was the cutbank across the alley from my house. In 1975 I got a job as a human rights worker at the Cariboo Friendship Centre. My role was to help people snagged in the system and make sure they were aware of their legal rights. Very little could compete with the addictions engulfing the Troopers. Then one cold winter day over the Christmas break, the opportunity presented itself for the Troopers and me to form an alliance. For the next year and a half we got to learn more about one another on a human basis. My first group of stories is about them.

EMILY LULUA EKKS

In 1977 I moved to a trapline in the Chilcotin near Tatla Lake. One day I bumped into Donald Lulua, a Tŝilhqot'in man I knew from Williams Lake, and he introduced me to his mother, Emily Lulua Ekks, and her husband, Donald Ekks. I soon realized the Elder couple, then in their sixties, were my neighbours.

Emily and Donald Ekks lived traditionally in a number of locations over a broad stretch of territory between Tatla Lake and Nemiah Valley.

Emily spoke little English, but Donald was conversant and willingly shared his stories. Emily was the mother of eight children and also raised two of her grandchildren despite being a single parent for much of her life. What made it work was her large extended family of four brothers and four sisters and many aunts, uncles and cousins who stood by her. Emily had a strong support network.

The Lulua clan occupied the region between Tatlayoko Valley and Tsuniah Lake, known as Naghatalhchuẑ or Big Eagle Lake (Choelquoit Lake) country. Donald Ekks helped raise Emily's last child, David, and her grandsons James and Patrick Lulua. Emily and Donald's principal summer residence was at Gwedzin or Cochin Lake with its spectacular backdrop of the sacred ?Eniyud mountain. They also had winter quarters in a small cabin closer to Tatla Lake. The miracle of Emily and Donald was how they managed to maintain their traditional Tŝilhqot'in lifestyle in the midst of modern society swirling about them.

THE HAYNES FAMILY OF TATLAYOKO

The story of the Haynes family offers a non-Indigenous perspective to the same territory occupied by the Lulua clan. Del Naomi Haynes brought four of her five sons to Tatlayoko Valley in the spring of 1930 to run the post office for K.B. Moore, a pioneer rancher and owner of Circle X Ranch. Lou Haynes was fifteen when they arrived and his brother Laurie was nine. Harry, seventeen, was already living in the Chilcotin at Alexis Lakes. Here we experience the Chilcotin through the lives of the brothers Harry, Lou and Laurie and their mother, Del Naomi Haynes, as told by her foster niece Bev Butler.

LUCY DAGG DESTER SULIN

Lucy Dagg and her first husband, Baptiste Dester, both had absentee white fathers and Tŝilhqot'in mothers. Despite growing up as Tŝilhqot'in, they were disenfranchised from their Indigenous status because of their paternity. At least that's one story.

Lucy and Baptiste lived together at Kleena Kleene and then Anahim Lake. Lucy and her second husband, Willie Sulin, made their home at Towdystan.

It's interesting how our lives connected. In April 1976 I drove to Kleena Kleene hauling my horse so I could ride down the Klinaklini Valley to visit friends living there. I got to Kleena Kleene late in the day and needed a place to spend the night. That's where I ran into thirteen-year-old Larry Sulin, the oldest grandchild of Willie and Lucy Sulin. Larry was attending the one-room Kleena Kleene School and was staying with his cousin Garry Gregg in a small house behind the school. He didn't hesitate to invite me to spend the night.

Two years later Lucy Sulin offered refuge to Chris Gilman, who had snowshoed out of the bush behind Towdystan to Lucy's house. She was on her way to live with me. Chris was leaving her husband and nine-year-old son behind and was trekking (hitchhiking and snowshoeing) to my trapline 160 kilometres away. Lucy had gone through a similar marriage breakup forty years earlier when she left Baptiste Dester and moved in with Willie Sulin, so she could identify with the gravity of Chris's undertaking. She didn't hesitate to give Chris shelter her first night out on the trail.

Five years later Lucy helped inspire my journalism career when she rode into our tent camp at Kleena Kleene on horseback. Lucy was in her late seventies by this time and had ridden three hours from Towdystan to Thelma's store at Clearwater Lake to buy a sack of flour. I felt the incident deserved documentation and managed to persuade *Williams Lake Tribune* editor Diana French to give me an old camera to capture such moments.

THE EDWARDS FAMILY OF LONESOME LAKE

When I came to the Cariboo Chilcotin Coast in 1973, the Edwards family of Lonesome Lake were cultural heroes and a household name both locally and across the United States. Leland Stowe's 1957 book *Crusoe of Lonesome Lake* saw to that. Ralph Edwards, the family patriarch, died in the fall of 1977, just as I was taking up residence on my Chilcotin trapline in the mountains south of Tatla Lake. His wife, Ethel, died shortly after that. But in August 1978 I met their oldest child, Stanley Edwards, on the trail to Lonesome Lake. Stanley was moving his herd of horned Ayrshire cattle up the valley to summer pasture at Stillwater Lake, where he had a cabin. Unlike ranchers in the Chilcotin, where cowboys rode horses, Stanley moved his cattle by foot.

Chris Gilman, who had changed her name to Yarrow Coldwater by that time, and I were visiting Wayne and Sie Padgett and their two kids, Jessib and Quimma. They were living in an old homestead beside the Atnarko River, a few kilometres up the Tote Road from the Bella Coola Highway, so Stanley was familiar with the place. He arrived at nightfall, just in time for supper, and spent the night camped in the barn with his herd of cattle tied to the fence, each cow with its own tether securely tied to a fence rail. Always unorthodox, Stanley wore his usual attire, a yellow hard hat and gumboots.

Years later I met Ralph and Ethel Edwards's second son, John, at his canoe camp on Turner Lake. It was 1993, and my two sons and I rented a canoe from him so we could paddle the Turner Lake portage chain. We also purchased some of his world-famous cinnamon buns and enjoyed his much talked about pancake breakfast. A few years later John and I were both fire wardens with the BC Forest Service. I fondly remember him giving his somewhat unorthodox weather reports from Lonesome Lake over the Forest Service radio. Sadly his vigilance for keeping a lookout for wildfires went unheeded in 2004, when a lightning strike started a small blaze on the steep slopes below Turner Lake. This happened on June 21, and BC Parks and the BC Forest Service chose to let it burn. A month later the fire turned into a raging inferno that consumed the Edwards family homestead on Lonesome Lake and caused catastrophic damage on the Chilcotin Plateau around Charlotte Lake. Author Chris Czajkowski writes about this travesty in her 2006 book *Wildfire in the Wilderness*.

I knew Trudy Turner, the youngest of the three Edwards children, a bit better. She and her husband, Jack Turner, moved from Lonesome Lake to a sunny location in the Bella Coola Valley in the late 1980s. Their daughter Susan Turner is a friend. Trudy was a regular competitor in the Bella Coola Gymkhana, a horseback riding competition often held in conjunction with the annual Bella Coola Rodeo.

What I found significant about the Edwards family story was how little contact or interface they had with the local Indigenous community. They were isolated, self-contained and fiercely independent.

TOMMY WALKER

In contrast to the Edwards family, Englishman Tommy Walker became well integrated with the Indigenous community of Ulkatcho from Anahim Lake, and later with the Telkwa People of northern British Columbia. Shortly after arriving in the Bella Coola Valley from England in 1929, Tommy initiated the first rodeo in the country, at his place in Stuie beside the Atnarko River, which drew competitors and spectators from across the Chilcotin and the Bella Coola Valley. A few years later this event morphed into the now-famous Anahim Lake Stampede sixty kilometres away on the Chilcotin Plateau.

Tommy was a strong promoter of Tweedsmuir Provincial Park, established in 1937, and became friends with British author John Buchan, Canada's fifteenth Governor General. In 1935 Buchan was elevated to the British peerage as the first Baron Tweedsmuir by King George V. Lord Tweedsmuir became an exemplary representative of the Crown, promoting Canada's cultural diversity and Indigenous sovereignty.

THE NUXALK-DAKELH GREASE TRAIL

Eulachon season was in full swing when I came to the Bella Coola Valley for the first time in the spring of 1973. Grease-making camps were set up along the lower part of the Bella Coola River near its mouth, and it was a hub of activity. Eulachon are sea-run smelt that spawn in glacier-fed rivers along the northwest coast of North America. They were a cultural key-stone species of the coastal Indigenous people because of the polyunsaturated fish oil that could be extracted from the high fat content of the fish. Eulachon grease was a highly sought-after trade item, and the trails from the coast into the interior were known as grease trails. One of the best-known grease trails in British Columbia was the Nuxalk-Dakelh Grease Trail from Bella Coola to the Fraser River. This route gained nationwide recognition because Scottish explorer Alexander Mackenzie followed it on his cross-continental journey in 1793.

Historically Mackenzie has been recognized as the first European to cross North America by land north of Mexico. As the bicentennial of this event grew closer in 1993, members of the Southern Dakelh Nation were concerned that the identity of their ancient travel route was being overshadowed by the colonial process. Their name for the trail, the Nuxalk-Dakelh Grease Trail, was being replaced by the name Alexander Mackenzie Heritage Trail. As a result, the Ulkatcho First Nation of Anahim Lake published the community's own record of events along the trail in the 1993 booklet *Ulkatcho Stories of the Grease Trail*.

This chapter reflects on the living history of Ulkatcho, Dakelh and Nuxalk people along the trail and offers a perspective on the importance of eulachon grease to the whole region. Andy Siwallace gives a delightful description of the grease-making process in excerpts borrowed from *Ulkatcho Stories of the Grease Trail*.

ANDY AND LILLIAN SIWALLACE

The book concludes with Andy and Lillian Siwallace sharing stories of their lives and struggles in Bella Coola to reinvigorate the Nuxalk culture after decades of suppression by the Canadian government. On the Central Coast, the United Church was handed the responsibility of indoctrinating Indigenous children against their culture. Somehow Andy and Lillian managed to straddle both realities, as leaders of Emmanuel United Church in Bella Coola and as strong adherents of their Nuxalk culture, bringing back their language and traditions.

THUNDER BERT AND THE
TROOPERS OF WILLIAMS LAKE

At the end of December 1975 I was clumping through the snow to my office in the Cariboo Friendship Centre when I came upon Thunder Bert Johnson trying to get into the building. Normally the facility was open, with its perpetual pot of coffee and soft sofas offering respite from the cold, but this day it was closed over the Christmas break. It was nearly −20°C, and Bert was cold and hungry.

Bert and his wife, Adele, were members of the Trooper community that frequented the streets of Williams Lake in those days and were regulars at the Friendship Centre. They lived in a derelict house known as the Troopers' Shack on a parcel of T'exelc First Nation (Sugar Cane) land within the city boundaries near Scout Island at the west end of Williams Lake. The property fronted on an extensive marsh at the outflow of the lake, and the house was owned by Sonny Gilbert, a member of T'exelc First Nation. Sonny shared his domain with up to a dozen other Indigenous people from various communities across the region.

How the Troopers got their name isn't exactly clear. There's some debate about it. Some say it was because of the way they moved about the city in group formation, following a wine jug down the alleys. Others say it had more to do with their cohesive identity, camaraderie and tendency to look out for one another like soldiers in a battalion. At any rate, it was an identity they readily embraced. They were defiant, perhaps, at being outcasts, but self-possessed with a devil-may-care attitude, not caring what others thought of them. They'd find a discreet location like a vacant lot or cutbank away from public scrutiny, and they'd sit down together and pass the jug around until it was empty. In the small cow town of Williams Lake, many residents and business owners alike knew them on a first-name basis. They had a history with the place and families who cared for them.

Writer and former *Williams Lake Tribune* editor Diana French once described the Troopers as people who had been displaced by technology. A decade or two earlier, the great ranches of the Cariboo Chilcotin had relied on a big pool of workers to cut and stack their hay using teams of horses pulling mowers, hay rakes and wagons. They'd use derrick poles to build gargantuan stacks of loose hay that weighed several tonnes each.

Large extended families of Indigenous people took hay-cutting contracts with various ranches, and the work would last several months depending on the size of the ranch and the weather. This work fit into their other seasonal activities such as hunting, fishing, trapping and gathering resources from the land, or other contract work like fence building, log cabin construction and cutting firewood.

Then the ranches started automating. Tractors replaced horses, and square balers, bread loaf stackers and eventually round balers replaced the need for large hay crews. So the Troopers had a skill set that was no longer required or valued, and many drifted to the urban places to find work. Some got stuck there. Alcohol was a big factor. That's how it was with Second World War vet Thunder Bert and his wife, Adele. Bert got the nickname Thunder because of his booming voice and outspoken manner. In his prime he was a physically powerful man. Now in his mid-sixties, he was somewhat diminished but still a capable worker.

Bert and Adele were from Esk'et (Alkali Lake), a Secwépemc community fifty kilometres south of Williams Lake along the Dog Creek Road. The couple had their own space staked out in Sonny Gilbert's Troopers' Shack, with a mattress on the floor and blankets and bags of clothing and personal belongings piled nearby.

The derelict building had no electricity or running water but was kept warm thanks to a wood-fired barrel heater turned on its side, which was also used for cooking. The rounded top of the barrel had been pounded flat to accommodate pots for cooking or heating water. Sometimes people cooked food inside the barrel over coals when the fire was low. An outhouse provided toilet facilities, and household water was dipped from the nearby marsh and strained through mosquito netting, and preferably boiled before consumption.

For the past year I'd worked as a human rights street worker out of the Friendship Centre. The Williams Lake Human Rights and Civil Liberties Association partnered with the Cariboo Friendship Society to fund the position. I spent a lot of time attending court, making sure people had legal representation, and helping people snagged in the bureaucracy to fill out the paperwork to get the services they were entitled to. My year's contract was almost over, and I had been offered a more formal position as a legal information worker. That would mean becoming a paralegal employed by the provincial government, but becoming a civil servant was the furthest thing from my mind. Earlier that year I'd bought a trapline and had ambitions to drop out of society and live in the bush. There was a groundswell of young people at that time "going back to the land."

Seeing Thunder Bert frustrated in his attempt to get out of the cold gave me an idea. He was broke and his next welfare cheque wasn't due for a while, so I asked if he was interested in cutting firewood to earn a few bucks. His immediate response was yes. I had the use of a three-ton truck and a chainsaw, so I took him back to the Troopers' Shack and asked if there were others who wanted to get into the firewood business. Enthusiasm was high and five or six volunteered, saying they'd be willing to go the next day. So that's how it started. I handed in my resignation and told my employers I wasn't going to pursue the civil servant job, and I launched our new business venture.

Members of our crew fluctuated depending on who was up for working. Usually there were five or six. Besides Bert and Adele, the core group included Charlie Casimer (also known as Charlie Charlie or Charlie Eye), his brother Billy Casimer, Peter "Sleepy" Alphonse (Charlie's sidekick), Robert Gilbert, Sonny Gilbert, Duncan Amut, Stanley Peters, Clara Bob, Ernie Bob, Muldeen Whitey and Tommy Wycotte.

The local sawmills had cull piles of dry logs that were too rotten, big or gnarly to go through their processing facility, and the Lignum sawmill gave us permission to cut their culls for firewood. Most of the Troopers knew folks who needed firewood, so we had no shortage of customers.

The undisputed leader among the Troopers was Tommy Wycotte, a Secwépemc man in his mid-fifties from Sugar Cane, the colloquial name for T'exelc First Nation, at the opposite end of Williams Lake from the city. I'd met Tommy Wycotte nearly two years earlier in the spring of 1974 on a tree-planting job with the Ministry of Forests. They hired maybe two dozen of us and paid us by the hour. The managers divided us into three crews: the white men in one crew, the white women in another crew and a crew of Indigenous planters. Then they tried to get the crews to compete against one another. Tommy was the obvious leader of the Indigenous crew. I remember him showing up for work in the morning with his devil-may-care attitude, somewhat hungover, waiting for the crummy to pick us up. What stood out most was his foot attire, a pair of caulk boots without laces. None of us non-Indigenous planters even had caulk boots, but at least our boots had laces. I remember the Forest Service bosses coming over to our crew planting on the sidehill and chiding us because the other two crews, the women and the Indigenous men, were planting way more trees than we were. We were slow and methodical and probably averaged 300 trees a day each. The women planted a similar number, but the Indigenous group led by Tommy Wycotte averaged a whopping 1,200 trees each. Of course we were paid by the hour and not by the tree, so we didn't have much incentive to work any faster. But Tommy, wearing boots without laces, quadrupled our production.

On our firewood-cutting project, Tommy usually operated the chainsaw while others split the big rounds and loaded them into the truck. We delivered wood to places around town and farther afield to

Deep Creek (thirty kilometres north), Lac la Hache (sixty kilometres south) and Riske Creek (fifty kilometres west). I would take a couple of crew members to deliver the wood and unload the truck, while Tommy and others continued cutting, splitting and piling the wood in the mill yard. At the end of the day we'd cook up a big meal at my place and share it together. It was too perfect, really, and I started entertaining the fantasy that we had somehow stumbled on the cure for chronic alcohol addiction, because it seemed their preoccupation with chasing a wine jug had somehow dissipated. Of course I was naive, and my learning curve was about to experience a sharp upward trajectory.

Our daily routine consisted of me driving down to the Troopers' Shack in the morning, picking up those who wanted to work, heading off to Lignum's cull pile and then delivering firewood to customers. This day, Tommy Wycotte didn't join us. It was curious, but I didn't think too much about it. Charlie Casimer, despite his glass eye, could sharpen and operate the chainsaw proficiently, so I left him in charge and took off with a couple of workers to make a delivery at Soda Creek. When we got back, Tommy had shown up and had resumed his usual role running the chainsaw. But something wasn't right. He was dishevelled, his hard hat tipped to one side, and he was standing off balance with one hand on the saw screaming full throttle through a 1.2-metre-diameter Douglas fir log. Suddenly things became clear. Tommy's absence that morning was explained. It was Welfare Wednesday, and he'd received his stipend from the government and had purchased a forty-pounder (a forty-ounce or 1.14-litre bottle) of whisky and brought it to our workplace. The rest of the crew was tipsy too, so that was it for our workday.

We continued our woodcutting campaign throughout the winter but had to implement a few guidelines. This included no booze while working. At some point I think I conceded to purchasing a small bottle of wine at the end of the day to share with our evening meal, but that's about it. We divvied up the income from our wood sales so the truck got a share, the saw got a share, and the workers and I split the rest.

"NOW HE'S COME BACK FOR THE ROCKS"

Charlie Casimer had three names: Charlie Charlie, Charlie Eye and Charlie Casimer. It wasn't unusual for Indigenous people to have two names in those days. People often took their father's first name as their last name, only to have official record keepers give them their father's last name for a surname. So it was with brothers Charlie and Billy Casimer. Their dad was Charlie Casimer, so they often went by Charlie Charlie and Billy Charlie. Then, to complicate things further, Charlie Charlie lost an eye through some unfortunate accident. How it happened I never heard, but he received a glass eye fitted into his eye socket. Hence his descriptor name, Charlie Eye.

When I first came to Williams Lake in 1973, I lived communally with a group of friends in three shacks at 280 North Mackenzie Avenue. In our attempt to survive and stretch a dollar, we regularly "shopped" in the big white bin disposal containers behind the grocery stores and brought home cartloads of expired but quite palatable food. Our property backed onto an alley that ran between Mackenzie Avenue and First Avenue North, and across the alley from our house was the service entrance to Famous Bakery, owned by Ole Henriksen. Ole often had day-old products we could get at half price. The Troopers visited the bakery too, hitting Ole up for his day-old products. Often they had no money so they would prevail on his good graces for items he might give them for free.

Ole told me Charlie Eye was one of his regulars. He said Charlie always had a sob story to soften him up, especially if he was broke. One of his favourite tricks for gaining sympathy was to pluck out his glass eye and hold it up as evidence of his misfortune. Ole said whenever he saw Charlie reaching for his glass eye, he'd stop him mid-sentence. "That's okay, Charlie, have some bread. Have a bag of cinnamon buns!"

Charlie Eye had a sharp wit and a poignant sense of irony. In the early 1970s Gibraltar Mines came to town and opened its copper and gold mine near McLeese Lake, just a few kilometres up the highway from Charlie's home community of Xatśūll. Charlie had a guttural voice because of an injury to his vocal cords and always spoke with drama and great intention. His classic comment about Gibraltar Mines was short and to the point: "The white man took our land. Now he's come back for the rocks."

The three-ton Dodge truck played a significant role in forging a link between the Troopers and what can only be described as a colourful chapter in Cariboo history. The truck was owned by a communal group of back-to-the-landers along the Horsefly Road east of Williams Lake. They called themselves Ochiltree Organic Commune. When I first met them in 1973, they owned a small acreage on the shores of Rose Lake, halfway between 150 Mile House and Horsefly. The group was headed by Jerry and Nancy LeBourdais, both in their late forties, who had abandoned a comfortable lifestyle in North Vancouver several years earlier to take up a communal life in the Cariboo. Jerry had had a well-paying job at the Shell oil refinery in Burnaby and was a labour activist and avowed communist. Nancy had worked as a nurse in a hospital. Around 1971 they had sold their house in the city and given up their careers to follow their dreams. Nancy said that on their journey north Jerry had tossed his wristwatch off the cliff at Jackass Mountain in the Fraser Canyon, insisting he'd be operating on a different time schedule from then on.

In his activism Jerry insisted that a true communist needed to live on a commune. They had a blended family that included Nancy's son Raymond and Jerry's daughter Linda and son Louie, all in their early twenties, and Lorraine, the teenage daughter they had together. Besides their own kids, several idealistic young people had also joined their pilgrimage from North Vancouver to form the commune.

In 1975 Jerry and Nancy sold their small farm on Rose Lake and moved lock, stock and barrel to an isolated homestead on the Borland Meadow owned by a local man, Willie Wiggins. The Borland Meadow was a big wild grass meadow a dozen kilometres off the Horsefly Road up a seasonally impassable wagon road. It was off the power grid, so the group needed a place to store their truck where the engine block could be plugged in during winter. They also required someone to haul ranch supplies out to them from Williams Lake on a regular basis, and that's where I came in. I kept the truck at my place in Williams Lake, where it could be plugged in when temperatures dropped. When it wasn't needed to haul stuff for the commune, I had free use of it to haul firewood.

Once a week or so, I'd drive big loads of wheat, oats, barley, hen scratch, building supplies, hay or whatever they needed to the end of the Borland Meadow road in Miocene. Meanwhile the commune had purchased a team of big Percheron horses, Meg and Maud, from Lester Dorsey in Anahim Lake, and Rod Henniker took on the role as teamster. He'd be waiting with the horses and wagon, or sleigh in winter, and would load up with as much weight as he figured the horses could pull. Often I'd ride into the Borland with him and spend the night. The next day we'd come out for another load and I'd take the empty truck back to town.

One day I brought Bert and Adele with me on the rendezvous to meet Rod. They rode into the Borland Meadow on the wagon and ended up spending several days there. It amazed me how the Elders from Esk'et came alive in the commune environment. Every time a squirrel would chirp in the trees, Adele would joke to Bert, "There's a dollar." She told us how they used to shoot squirrels by the hundreds back home and get a few cents apiece for them. It was a way of life they had known from childhood, and how they made their money.

Bert and Adele started a trend that other Troopers followed, and the commune welcomed the extra help and expertise. It was a perfect fit, really, because most of the communards were young urban idealists in their early twenties bent on learning back-to-the-land skills. The Troopers had first-hand knowledge of haying with horses, building Russell fences, building log cabins and feeding animals. The commune had a mixed farm with a menagerie of animals, including pigs, chickens, ducks, geese, horses, goats, sheep, beef cows, milk cows and of course dogs and cats. For the Troopers, a stay on the commune gave them a welcome respite from the street. There was no pay involved, but they got plenty of good food

The CEEDS (Community Enhancement and Economic Development Society) work crew harvesting potatoes on Tommy Wycotte's land at Sugar Cane. Left to right are Jerry LeBourdais, Willy Hurst, Harriet Tenale, Lorraine LeBourdais, Tommy Wycotte, Tony Bob, Rosie Laceese, Ernie Bob, Terry Peters and Gussie Williams. Photo courtesy CEEDS

and rest and healthy activity, and their skills were valued and appreciated. Then when the street called out to them, they'd head back into town.

Jerry and Nancy were the de facto leaders of the group, though they insisted that everyone was equal. They were older and had sacrificed the most to make the commune a reality. After all, it was the sale of their property and their life savings that financed the operation to keep this great social experiment going. But officially there was no hierarchy. Jerry had a vision of a network of rural agricultural communes spread across the landscape to replace the capitalist system. It was a pipe dream, quite literally. Great discussions would ensue after toking copious joints of homegrown in the Borland Meadow headquarters cabin, where chickens regularly made their way inside and laid eggs in the woodbox.

The commune's use of the Borland Meadow was by the good graces of Willie Wiggins, whose grandfather Jimmy Wiggins had purchased it in 1911. Besides the rustic log cabin and barn, the group set up several wall tents with log sides heated by airtight wood heaters to accommodate everyone. Besides a share of the Borland Meadow with a neighbouring ranch, there were several other meadows that could be used for cutting hay or pasture. The loose barter arrangement with Willie included feeding his small herd of cows and providing sides of pork, bacon and other products like eggs and vegetables from the garden. Plans were made to expand the operation by building a two-storey log dormitory to house the many guests who were gravitating to the scene.

Dinah Belleau joined up with Ochiltree Organic Commune in 1977 while the group was farming with the Troopers on Tommy Wycotte's land at Sugar Cane. She lived with the commune, which later rebranded itself as CEEDS, for twenty years. Then in the late 1990s she returned to her home in Esk'et (Alkali Lake), where she started a big community garden and passed on organic gardening knowledge to her own people. Liz Twan photo

Jerry put the word out asking if there were any carpenters in the Trooper crowd. As it happened, Tommy Wycotte's older brother, Jimmy Wycotte, was a builder. He lived in a two-storey lumber-frame house he'd constructed himself at the edge of the Sugar Cane reserve. And Jimmy knew another Secwépemc man, Willie Tappage from Deep Creek, who had carpentry skills. Deep Creek was part of Xatśūll Northern Secwépemc First Nation, twenty kilometres north of town. Willie's sister, Augusta Evans, had recently become a celebrity thanks to the 1973 book *The Days of Augusta*, by Jean E. Speare, and the brilliant photography of Robert Keziere. Willie lived with Augusta in her small log cabin beside Highway 97.

Both Jimmy and Willie agreed to go to work for the commune. I drove them out to rendezvous with Rod and the horses, and they rode into the meadow on the wagon. A couple of months later, the new two-storey structure was finished. Jimmy, sixty-six, and Willie, well into his seventies, were Elders, so the heavy lifting was left to the energetic young communards. Other Troopers also continued to come out and spend a few days or even weeks at a time at the commune. Some, such as Dinah Belleau, Gussie Williams, Marvin Bob and Ernie Bob, became permanent members and spent years with the group.

Meanwhile the commune was expanding. A satellite camp was set up at the old Miocene schoolhouse on the Horsefly Road a short distance from the end of the Borland Meadow road. This became the group's main pig-raising operation with several sows and a boar. They sold weaner pigs in the spring and pork throughout the year.

I spent the summer of 1976 living with the commune at the Borland Meadow. My main job was looking after the greenhouse attached to the south side of the barn. Essentially it was a geodesic dome–like structure framed with small aspen poles and covered with plastic. I stayed on through the fall. Then in December I got an urgent request over the local radio message service to contact the Cariboo Friendship Centre. Long story short, I got hired to run a temporary shelter in Williams Lake for Indigenous people who had come to town from outlying communities and didn't have a place to stay. A man had been found frozen to death in a snowbank the year before, so the city and the provincial government set up a couple of Avco trailers as emergency accommodation. The trailers sat on vacant land next to the Cariboo Friendship Centre, and we called it the Time Out Shelter. Most of our clients were from out west of the Fraser River in the Chilcotin or Blackwater country.

Word got out about our warm, cozy place, and our twenty beds were usually full. We were supposed to impose a three-night limit on our guests, but some folks stayed longer if there was room and if they pitched in and helped out. We provided two meals a day and stayed closed during the day when the Friendship Centre was open. This was my introduction to members of the Tŝilhqot'in and Dakelh communities: Percy Hink, a former Chief of Yuneŝit'in; Euphrasia Williams, an Elder and storyteller from Tŝideldel; Duncan Amut and Muldeen Whitey from Yuneŝit'in; Agnes Chantyman from Lhoosk'uz; Rosie Laceese from Tl'esqox; Donald Lulua from Tŝideldel; and Ivan Solomon from Xeni Gwet'in.

"MY SÉME7"

Duncan Amut was a Tŝilhqot'in man who was in his forties when I met him on the streets of Williams Lake. In his younger days Duncan had known success in the rodeo arena. He was from Yuneŝit'in, known then as Stoney, and had drifted into town and never left. He was close friends with Sonny Gilbert and resided at the Troopers' Shack. Both Sonny and Duncan were diminutive men and quite jovial, especially when nursing a beer together in the Maple Leaf Hotel pub.

One day I was walking with Duncan down the main drag of Williams Lake when he stopped in front of a business on Oliver Street and said, "That's my *séme7*. That's where he works."

Séme7, pronounced *sem-mah*, with an abrupt glottal stop indicated by the numeral 7, is the Secwépemc term for "white man." Duncan of course was Tŝilhqot'in, but when in Rome, do as the Romans. Residing in the unceded territory of the Secwépemc, Duncan gave preference to the local vernacular. More to the point, he was giving me an education on survival on the streets. Duncan explained that when he got his social assistance cheque at the end of the month, he'd take it to his friend in the store, who would cash it for him.

Then he'd get the guy to give him just a few dollars at a time and keep the balance in an envelope in the cash register. Whenever Duncan needed some money, he'd go see his *séme7* and get five or ten dollars until his cache was used up. His *séme7* was his banker, trusted friend and confidant. This was an essential street-smart survival technique, because folks living on the street often didn't have ID and would have a hard time cashing their cheques at the bank. Or if they did manage to cash their cheques, they likely didn't have bank accounts, so that would mean packing their whole grubstake in their pocket, making them vulnerable to getting rolled.

The way Duncan spoke the phrase "my *séme7*" conveyed a relationship of friendship, trust and respect. That's my *séme7*, my special friend who helps me out and has my back.

When the weather got warmer in March, the Time Out facility closed, and I rented a four-bedroom house with Percy Hink, Jimmy Wycotte and a couple of others who had become regulars at the shelter. We agreed to make the place an alcohol-free refuge and kept busy doing a few useful projects around town. One of these was to fix up Sonny Gilbert's Troopers' Shack.

Street people with no fixed address who didn't pay rent received only the food portion of their provincial welfare stipend. If they could show rental receipts, they were entitled to substantially more money. We managed to convince the Ministry of Social Services to cough up the rental portion for several Troopers staying in Sonny Gilbert's abode so we could make improvements to its dilapidated condition. Thunder Bert and Adele Johnson, Charlie Charlie, Sleepy (Peter Alphonse), Billy Casimer, Stanley Peters, Clara Bob and Tommy Wycotte agreed to let their names be used to trigger this extra money, which was paid directly to us. Then we hired Percy and Jimmy to make the repairs and purchased building materials. We worked together to put on new asphalt rolled roofing, repaired broken glass windows by replacing them with Plexiglas, and laid new vinyl flooring. We had enough funds to purchase a new wood cookstove, a new stovepipe and a new wood heater.

Meanwhile I hired Percy and Jimmy to build a couple of plywood storage containers for my pending exodus to my trapline in the Chilcotin. They trimmed them with sheet metal along the edges to keep mice and other intruders from gnawing into my cache.

One day in early spring 1977, Tommy Wycotte took me aside and told me he had property at the Sugar Cane reserve at the east end of Williams Lake, beside the San Jose River, that was good for growing a garden. As a young man, he had raised his family on the produce he grew there. Since I was leaving town soon it wasn't something I wanted to pursue, so I suggested we talk to the folks at Ochiltree Organic Commune to see if they'd be interested. Tommy had been out to the Borland Meadow several times and liked what he saw there, so we set up a meeting to discuss the idea. Tommy said the group could use the big garden site and nearby pasture for a milk cow and other animals. It meant a radical shift in the commune's focus. After careful consideration, the group decided to accept Tommy's offer. Big wall tents were set up for accommodation, fences were built to contain the animals, and the garden area was plowed, fenced and planted.

That's how it was when I left Williams Lake in June 1977 for the Chilcotin. I spent twenty-four years in the west country and would come to town two or three times a year for business or shopping. On one of these occasions I spotted Tommy Wycotte with a group of friends, and he immediately stepped forward and thrust out his hand. The deal with the commune using his land had worked out to his satisfaction, and we shook hands. Somehow the eye contact and firm grip of friendship resonated with us both.

Some years later I heard Tommy died tragically. Hit by a car while walking down the highway, I was told. But that was Tommy's way. Living on the edge, following the dictates of his own calling, walking to the beat of his own drum.

When I moved back to Williams Lake in 2001 to take a job with the *Williams Lake Tribune*, I met Tommy's daughter Marge Wycotte living on the streets. I think Tommy had pointed her out to me many years earlier, so I knew who she was. She'd spot you in the Save-On-Foods parking lot and unabashedly come forward and hit you up for a donation to her cause. We often talked about Tommy and her family. I didn't know Marge's circumstances or why she ended up the way she did, but physically she was the spitting image of her dad. Sometimes, if I had a loonie or two in my

Tommy Wycotte holds his granddaughter Renee Wycotte in approximately 1974. Chris Wycotte photo

Marge Wycotte was the spitting image of her dad, Tommy Wycotte, both in appearance and her free and generous spirit. Photo courtesy Chris Wycotte

pocket, I'd offer her a token of help.

Like her dad, Marge was a survivor. I remember on a cold winter evening outside the grocery store meeting Marge gorging on an open can of oysters. She was hungry and was just using her fingers to stuff the oily prize into her mouth, devouring it with gusto and luxuriating in the rich and simple delicacy.

Another time I was picking up a friend at the Greyhound bus depot and saw Marge in there taking refuge from a cold winter afternoon. We talked briefly, and she told me her family didn't approve of her way of life and that she was maybe going to quit drinking.

"But I don't want other people telling me what to do," she said. "I don't care what they think."

Just then a young woman burst out the door of the adjoining restaurant and walked over to Marge and gave her a handful of change.

"Here you go, Auntie," she said.

That was the last time Marge and I visited. Then a few years later I spotted her outside Deni House, the extended care facility next to Cariboo Memorial Hospital.

"Hi, Marge!" I called out.

"I'm not Marge," she retorted.

"What do you mean you're not Marge?" I questioned.

"I'm not Marge," she insisted.

And that was it. I never saw Marge again, and I started to doubt whether it had been she I had actually spoken to outside Deni House.

Heading home one day, I came across a couple in high-vis apparel in my neighbourhood, one riding a bike and the other jogging up the street. They had signs on their clothing, and I waved at them but didn't think much more about it.

Then, in the *Williams Lake Tribune* of September 30, 2021, there was an article titled "Running and Biking for Marge and Children." A couple

Troopers collage. Clockwise from top left: Robert Gilbert driving the dump-rake; Paulsie Alphonse playing the fiddle; sitting on the log, Dinah Belleau, Leslie Hurst, Wayne Ottie and Poncho Sandy, Big Chuck Cortourelli, Violet Ottie and Terry Peters; Johnny Bates with a bucket of potatoes; Ernie Bob, Stanley Peters, Clara Bob and Robert Jeff; Freddie Sampson and Samson Jack (a friend of CEEDS from Tl'esqox, but not a member of the Troopers community); Leslie Hurst driving the horse; Violet Ottie and Freddie Sampson carrying protest signs; Gussie Williams with a wheelbarrow of squash. In the centre, Tommy Wycotte and Rosie Laceese. Photo collage courtesy CEEDS

named James and Jackie Mattice were running and riding for the late Marge Wycotte, the article stated.

"We are also running for the children," James Mattice told reporter Monica Lamb-Yorski, "not only children from the past but in the future too."

They were wearing orange T-shirts with "Every Child Matters" emblazoned on the front and "Run for Sister Marge" on the back. The couple said they usually run to honour people who have passed on. Marge Wycotte, born in 1959, passed away September 22, 2021, at Deni House.

I posted a short piece on Facebook to commemorate Marge and acknowledge the newspaper article. Several people commented, but the response from Kim Kaytor bears repeating. Kim is owner of Smashin' Smoothies, a thriving business across the street from the Save-On-Foods where Marge hung out.

"Marge Wycotte was an angel walking among us!" stated Kim. "She was the only customer that successfully held a long time account with our business. She would come in for a hot cup of tea or a bowl of soup, but most of the time she was requesting a smoothie or soup for someone else that she knew was hungry and needed a good meal. At first I assumed we were making donations, but Marge insisted we keep track. She consistently came in once a month to pay her account in full and made sure to have a little extra for the staff.

"When I think of how the Creator wants us to treat and look out for our neighbours, I will forever remember Marge, her generous spirit and her loving heart. Always thinking of and looking out for others amidst her own struggles. RIP Marge!"

I contacted Kim to ask if we could include her message in this story.

"I've wanted people to know the good side of Marge for a long time," Kim replied. "Yes! I am so happy you are willing to share these stories. Thank you!"

Kim added, "I could go on and on about Marge! She was brilliant! It was easy for people to dislike her and look down on her because of her rough personality and her limp. Many people thought she was always drunk, but like her dad, Marge was also hit by a car and her leg had not healed properly."

She recalled one time she was giving Marge a ride home and pulled up at an intersection behind a car stopped for the red light.

"Hey," Marge said to Kim, "you're too close. You're supposed to stop far enough back that you can see where the tires on the vehicle in front of you touch the ground."

Kim said she looked at Marge astonished.

"Ha, you're right, Marge. How did you know that?" she asked.

Marge told her she had once had her driver's licence, so she'd better drive right.

"We both had a good laugh and Marge made sure I abided by the rules of the road the rest of the way home."

Kim said she and Marge shared many moments of laughter and tears over the years. Sometimes Marge would talk about her "evil twin"—a look-alike woman always getting her into trouble. Marge said she really wanted to meet this twin and tell her how much trouble she was causing her.

Then Kim told me about a young girl who came into Smashin' Smoothies one day while Marge was there.

"Marge was a bit gruff," Kim said, "which was often the case with her, but it didn't seem to bother the girl. Then the girl shared a story about how a group of guys had cornered her coming out of the movie theater late one night and she was scared and didn't have many options. Marge saw what was going on and lit into the guys and chased them off. Then she walked her to a safer spot. The girl had so much gratitude for what Marge had done for her that night, she didn't seem to mind that Marge didn't remember her."

To borrow a phrase from Duncan Amut, you could rightly say Kim was Marge's *séme7*.

Chris Wycotte, Tommy Wycotte's son and Marge's brother, and treaty manager for T'exelc (Williams Lake First Nation), told me he appreciated seeing something written about the Troopers that outlines the great qualities and value they had as people.

"My dad was a big part of that group," he said. "His love and his loyalty was invested in that group because it was a true brotherhood and sisterhood that you could not find anywhere else. I tried my best to get him off the streets, but to no avail. He felt more comfortable being among his friends.

"Most people saw them as degenerates, beaten-down and people of little value. Many of them in their own way were brilliant, humorous and caring people."

Then Chris corrected my misconception of Tommy's death.

"My dad was actually hit by a logging truck," he said. "I drove by the accident scene with my cousin Ernie, not realizing the person under the yellow tarp was my dad. I found out later that night when the RCMP came to my door and informed me of his death."

Chris added that he also appreciated having the positive side of his sister expressed.

"I can confirm that even though Marge was struggling with mental illness, she still had the ability to show compassion and caring for other people. She called me at work on a regular basis just to say hello and ask how I was doing."

DINAH BELLEAU DISCOVERS HER GREEN THUMB WITH CEEDS

Dinah Belleau was thirty-four years old when she came to live with Ochiltree Organic Commune on Tommy Wycotte's land at Sugar Cane. Dinah found a home with these idealistic communard hippies and stayed with them through the sometimes turbulent changes the group went through. She spent more than twenty years with the group as they moved to several locations around the Cariboo, Chilcotin and North Thompson and changed their name to Community Enhancement and Economic Development Society, better known by the acronym CEEDS. They set up a garden and animal husbandry operation at Tl'esqox (Toosey First Nation) for a season in Riske Creek. They had a couple of houses in the city of Williams Lake, then moved to Horse Lake and Lone Butte, where some members of the group still live today.

A rotating crew of Indigenous workers helped out at various times in the different locations. Troopers like Tommy Wycotte, Charlie Casimer, Billy Casimer, Clara Bob, Marvin Bob and Thunder Bert and Adele Johnson would spend time there, but they would inevitably head back to the streets of Williams Lake. Dinah said that when she was with the group at Sugar Cane, she didn't see Tommy Wycotte too much because he was usually hanging around town. But other Troopers like Ernie Bob and Gussie Williams, along with Dinah, spent more time with CEEDS than anyone else.

In her first years with the group, Dinah spent two summers herding sheep in the alpine above Crooked Lake east of Horsefly. Then she moved with the group to Horse Lake, where a great organic garden and potato patch got established.

In the late 1990s Dinah felt the urge to return to her home community of Esk'et.

"I felt guilty being away so long," she told me. "All the Elders and my friends were passing away, and I wanted to live with my own people. I'm thankful for the years I spent with CEEDS. I learned a lot and I'm thankful for that. Come to think of it, I enjoyed it at CEEDS, especially with the animals. Some are born and some die. I seen all that. I had lots of enjoyment with them. I had a good life with CEEDS."

Back at Esk'et, Dinah had the opportunity to use the expertise she had gained at CEEDS to help her own community. At some point she started a big organic garden project and began sharing all she knew with fellow community members, mentoring them with the skills she had picked up with CEEDS.

She knew where to order the best untreated seeds from the William Dam company, and she tried varieties of vegetables never grown in Esk'et before. She kept a record book to keep track of which varieties did best.

"I don't think the people at Esk'et like the colour purple," Dinah told Liz Twan in an article Liz wrote about the Esk'et garden for the *Williams Lake Tribune*'s 2008 summer supplement *Casual Country*. "Every purple thing I've ever grown in this garden has been hard to give away. I grew purple beans that actually turn green when you cook them, but no one wanted to eat them."[1]

Now, at seventy-eight years old, Dinah is retired and living in a seniors' housing apartment at Esk'et with her cat. She's a bit stove-up and doesn't get around like she used to anymore, and she hasn't gardened for a number of years. But she has no regrets. She has fond memories of her time with CEEDS and is grateful for the learning and experiences she gained there. It gave her something of value to bring home to her people, she said.

"I worked on the land as long as my bones would take it," she told me, laughing. "But I'm pretty slowed down now."

Rob Diether, one of the last remaining CEEDS members, still lives at Horse Lake near 100 Mile House. He said he still thinks about the Troopers all the time.

"You can't forget Marvin Bob," Rob told me. "He coined the phrase for the Trooper code of conduct: 'Chip in and share the wealth.'"

Rob figures the story of the Troopers was really a story of how the trauma of residential school and the entire experience of colonization impacted Indigenous Peoples.

"There was a lot of pain. They came out of residential school with little education. Their farming, ranching and living off the land skills they learned from their Elders. Tommy Wycotte used to say the only thing they learned at the mission was how to steal, because the kids were so damn hungry. I remember Sleepy [Peter Alphonse] saying he couldn't help it. Maybe he was trying to explain the state of his life. He probably felt shame."

Rob said Dinah Belleau more or less left the street scene after she joined CEEDS. Then she returned to her people empowered with skills she had acquired there.

"We were so honoured to have Dinah in our midst and to meet all the Troopers," Rob said. "They were an important part of our story."

---

1   This article was later included in the anthology *Gumption & Grit: Women of the Cariboo Chilcotin* (Caitlin Press, 2009).

EMILY LULUA EKKS

Donald Lulua walked with a limp. I met him around 1975 while I was employed as a street worker at the Cariboo Friendship Centre in Williams Lake. He was a regular there. He told me he had injured his leg when he got dragged by a horse as a kid out west in the Chilcotin, where he grew up. His foot got caught in the stirrup and there was no doctor or medical help to set his broken bones, so his leg never healed properly.

The Friendship Centre was a large two-storey house at the corner of Yorston Street and Third Avenue South where the modern Friendship Centre facility sits today. For decades that was the residence of the Indian agent, the federal government representative charged with enforcing the Indian Act on Indigenous reserves. But in the early 1970s, the Cariboo Friendship Society took it over as a welcoming place for Indigenous people who came to town from outlying communities. The coffee pot was always on.

I'd see Donald at various meetings or just sitting around drinking coffee. Then every once in a while he'd excuse himself and disappear. He'd say he had to go west to help his mother, and he'd be gone from the rigours of town life for several weeks at a time. Then he'd return. This intrigued me.

I knew very little about the Chilcotin in those days. To me the high plateau country west of the Fraser River was a mysterious place. Freedom exuded from the land. Once you crossed the Fraser River and started climbing Sheep Creek Hill, things felt different. Some people described it as a step back in time, a forgotten place, linked together by narrow winding roads and an undulating landscape where every twist and turn had a story.

When I met Donald, I was trying to make enough money to put a grubstake together so I could move to the trapline a friend and I had bought in the mountains south of Tatla Lake. Like many young people in those days, we were looking for a way to get back to the land. Finally in June 1977 I pulled up stakes in Williams Lake and headed out west. A short time later I ran into Donald at a funeral in Nimpo Lake.

Tŝilhqot'in patriarch Sam Sulin had passed away, and hundreds of people had gathered at his home at Fish Trap, where the Dean River

Sam Sulin, holding the reins of his horse and standing with Euphrasia Guichon Williams of Tŝideldel, was a respected Elder at Fish Trap, where the Dean River spills out of Nimpo Lake. Photo courtesy Euphrasia Guichon Williams

spills out of Nimpo Lake. Donald spotted me through the crowd and came right over. Then he began introducing me around to his family and friends and made me feel welcome.

The funeral customs of the Tŝilhqot'in and Dakelh Peoples were completely new to me. In my non-Indigenous world, funerals were short, sombre, private affairs. My dad had died the year before I moved to the Chilcotin, and the ceremony had been awkward, detached and insufficient. But here things were different. Everything stopped for a week or more as people showed up from across the region to celebrate the respected Elder. Projects on the go ceased. Hay cut in fields was left unattended. The pounding of nails and the buzzing of saws on building projects became silent.

A vigil fire burned around the clock in front of Sam's house, and an endless supply of food was prepared for the hundreds of guests who kept arriving over the three days I was there. People stopped by to console the grieving family. There was an informal casualness, an intimacy, a combination of tears and laughter, even revelry. Broken hearts were touched; spirits were mended. A key component to the celebration was the gambling: a string of lahal and poker games lasted into the wee hours of the morning.

Perhaps what impressed me most was the innate closeness of that far-flung community that stretched from the Fraser River to Bella Coola and from the southernmost Chilcotin Plateau to the Nechako and Blackwater watersheds. People came from Cheslatta, Burns Lake, Vanderhoof, Lhoosk'uz, Nazko, Quesnel, Williams Lake, Xeni Gwet'in, Chezacut, Bella Coola and farther afield. Someone shot a moose, and fresh salmon was brought up from Bella Coola as many people pitched in to cut up the meat and prepare the food for the continual feasting.

I later learned that Fish Trap was part of the Ulkatcho First Nation of Anahim Lake, and that the community was both Dakelh (Southern Carrier) and Tŝilhqot'in. The people at Fish Trap and farther down the road at Towdystan identified more as Tŝilhqot'in, but most of the people in Anahim Lake considered themselves Dakelh. It was complicated. Sam Sulin was Tŝilhqot'in, but his late wife, Mary, was Secwépemc, and several of their daughters had Dakelh husbands. Sam's father, Frank Sulin, was Tŝilhqot'in, but his mother, Ellie Stillas, was Dakelh, a sister to Baptiste Stillas, great-grandfather to revered Ulkatcho Chief Jimmy Stillas, who later made an impactful difference to the community. Then there were strong family ties to the Nuxalk of Bella Coola as well.

Because of this mix, the Dakelh from Lhoosk'uz and Nazko referred to their Ulkatcho neighbours as *Nechowt'en*, or "Dakelh mixed with Tŝilhqot'in." Despite occasional disputes arising from these differences, I learned to see *Nechowt'en* as an asset of diversity in the Ulkatcho community, not a liability.

At Sam Sulin's funeral Donald Lulua introduced me to his mother, Emily Lulua Ekks, and her husband, Donald Ekks. They lived in Naghatalhchuẑ or Big Eagle Lake (Choelquoit Lake) country between Tatla Lake and Nemiah Valley, more than 120 kilometres from Nimpo Lake. My trapline was 60 kilometres south of Tatla Lake, and I gradually came to realize that the old couple were my neighbours.

LAHAL: THE BONE GAME

In the ancient traditional gambling game of lahal, teams of half a dozen or more players face each other and attempt to outwit each other guessing in which hand the opposing players are holding the concealed striped and unstriped bones. While one team is guessing, the players on the team concealing the bones drum and sing to psychologically overpower their opponents. The stakes can be high with the winning team taking home a horse or cow or a saddle.

Lahal players Andrew Squinas, Marvin Paul, Sammy Lulua. Sage Birchwater photo

Emily and Donald Ekks lived the old-time way. They occupied several cabins and encampments throughout the year that weren't part of the federal government's "Indian reserve" system. And the places they lived weren't designated fee-simple lands, either, where they'd be obligated to pay taxes. They lived in places their ancestors had always occupied, and they moved with the seasons, harvesting the bounty from the land. Nobody, not even government minions, contested their right to be there.

Their winter quarters were a small cabin next to a spring about three or four kilometres out of Tatla Lake along the old Tatlayoko Road. Emily's youngest son, David Lulua, lived with them.

Another fifteen kilometres farther down the Tatlayoko Road, Emily and Donald had a second cabin on the shores of Gwedzin (Cochin) Lake. David Lulua and Emily's grandson James Lulua Sr. helped build it for them out of small-diameter logs when they were only fourteen and fifteen years old. This was Emily and Donald's summer abode, where they would set their gillnet in the lake to catch rainbow trout and suckers. What wasn't eaten fresh would be dried on racks over a smoky fire.

Few places are more stunningly beautiful than Gwedzin. Overshadowing the lake and cabin are the icy crags of ?Eniyud, a mountain of significance to the Tŝilhqot'in People. Here the Chilcotin Plateau interfaces with the Coast Mountains. Off in the distance to the south, the rounded Potato Mountains, known as Tŝimol Ch'ed, can be seen with the rugged peaks of the Coast Mountains poking up behind.

Emily's oldest son, Ubill, also had a cabin at Gwedzin, a couple hundred metres farther down the lake. It was a more posh affair with finished doors and windows and large enough to accommodate his family. Ubill and his wife, Julianna, lived most of the year at Xeni Gwet'in in Nemiah Valley, some eighty kilometres away, but like Emily and Donald, they occupied the whole of the landscape throughout the year. In late summer they maintained a large fishing camp at Henry's Crossing to harvest and dry sockeye and chinook salmon. Emily and Donald also camped there in sockeye season.

What grabbed my attention most was how Emily and Donald managed to survive in the midst of the busy settler society swirling about them. At one end of Gwedzin was a public campground; at the other end of the lake, a modern ranch. Just over the ridge from their place was a cultivated hay meadow.

Emily and Donald never owned a vehicle and neither of them had a driver's licence, but that didn't slow them down. Sure, Emily's kids, including Ubill, Minnie, Oggie, Raymond and occasionally David, had vehicles, but they weren't always around. When Emily and Donald wanted to go somewhere, they simply walked out to the Tatlayoko Road and waited patiently until somebody came along. The etiquette in the community was to stop and give them rides. Similarly in downtown Tatla Lake

Donald unabashedly approached people having coffee at the Graham Inn or picking up their mail at the post office, and he would ask if they had room to give them a lift home or perhaps to a different destination like Anahim Lake, Redstone, Williams Lake or Nemiah Valley.

"WE LIVE ALL OVER THIS LAND"

When I was still living in Williams Lake and doing the firewood project with the Troopers, one of our customers was Baptiste Meldrum of Riske Creek. Baptiste was a good-natured guy who had been out in the world more than many of his fellow Tŝilhqot'in. The agent to broadening his horizons was his success as a boxer. During the 1940s, '50s and '60s, boxing was a big deal in the Cariboo Chilcotin. Matches were regularly staged in Williams Lake, and Baptiste was a regular combatant. Apparently he fought big-name fighters farther afield and took so many blows to the head that he ended up punch-drunk. This neurodegenerative disorder can manifest as dementia, disorientation or confusion. Baptiste often seemed a bit dreamy and spaced out, but I always found him open and friendly.

I'd often see Baptiste and his wife standing by the side of the road, hitchhiking back and forth between Riske Creek and Williams Lake. If I had room I'd stop and give them a lift. Eventually the Meldrums got a place at a seniors' housing facility in Williams Lake and didn't have to make that fifty-kilometre commute.

At one point I mentioned to Baptiste my trapline near Tatla Lake, about two hundred kilometres west of his place at Riske Creek, and his response blew my mind.

"Tatla Lake is where I live too," he said. "The whole Chilcotin is my country, not just one place."

Then he told me the proper way to pronounce Tatla.

"*Taht-lah*," he said gently.

Baptiste had an understanding of the country that preceded colonization, and he knew where the various Tŝilhqot'in families had lived across the broad landscape before they were pushed out and displaced by settlers. This concept of living in the whole territory was completely new to me and foreign to my way of perceiving the world.

"*Nen gagunlhchugh deni nidlin*," he said. "We live all over this land."

Thanks to information provided by Lorraine Weir and Roger William that will be published in their upcoming book *Lha Yudit'ih We Always Find a Way: Bringing the Tŝilhqot'in Title Case Home* (Talon Books, 2022).

The couple also had a cabin at Tŝideldel on Redstone Flats, but they were seldom there. I owned a 1966 Chevy half-ton pickup with a flat deck and stock racks on the back. Even with my partner and two or more kids stuffed in the cab, we always managed to squeeze Emily and Donald in.

Emily and Donald's cabin at Gwedzin was only a kilometre or two off the main road, so it was an easy walk even in the worst weather for them to come and go. But driving in on the rugged track to their cabin was another matter. The road was unmaintained and quickly brought you to a different time and mindset. It was a natural speed bump between their slowed-down reality and the hyped-up urgency of the outside world. You had to drive slowly, preferably in low range. It gave you a chance to adjust your thinking and become more attuned to the lifestyle embraced by this traditional Tŝilhqot'in couple following the old ways of their culture.

I remember taking them home one time, idling through the ruts and potholes and bouncing over rocks in granny gear. Emily, very much alive to everything around her, excitedly pointed to an animal darting through the underbrush. "*Gex!*" she said to Donald, who kindly translated, "Rabbit." As we slowly inched along, he mentioned how a coyote had been up on the ridge above the cabin just yesterday. Then he pointed where a bear had crossed the road just two days earlier. And other times when there was nothing to say, Emily would start humming quietly to herself, the gentle sound of a person comfortable in her own skin.

There were other moments too. A lazy afternoon in the hot sun, old people sitting around in the high grass, and Donald Ekks introducing me to his sister Minnie, some twenty years his senior. She wanted a ride to Tatla Lake, he told me, so we bundled into my old red truck, some sitting in the cab, others comfortably perched on the flat deck behind. As we trundled over the gravel through the dust, I had a hard time imagining my own eighty-year-old grandmother so agile and at ease riding between the swaying stock racks.

In the spring of 1989 I got an invitation to visit Emily and Donald at Gwedzin. The archaeologist David Friesen was going to be there to demonstrate obsidian knapping with samples he'd collected from Besbut'a (Anahim Peak) near Anahim Lake. When we got there Donald was preparing a culinary feast of sucker fish stuffed with eggs, propped up on sticks and roasting beside the fire. It was a memorable occasion.

David shared the skills he had learned from Tahltan people near Mount Edziza—one of the only other places in British Columbia besides Besbut'a where obsidian is found. Whacking a fist-sized cobble of the volcanic glass with a piece of deer antler, David reduced it into smaller, flatter chunks, which he fashioned into sharp projectile points.

Emily Lulua Ekks at her Gwedzin camp, twenty kilometres south of Tatla Lake along the Tatlayoko Road. Sage Birchwater photo

Opposite: Donald Ekks with his single-shot .22 rifle, which he used for hunting squirrels, rabbits and grouse. Sage Birchwater photo

Donald Ekks pulls in a harvest of rainbow trout and suckers on Gwedzin Lake the morning after he and Emily Lulua Ekks set their gillnet. Sage Birchwater photo

These he processed further using the tip of the antler tine to press along the edges of the flattened, brittle rock. Soon he had it shaped into an arrowhead. His tool kit was simple: short pieces of deer antler and a thick piece of leather for a working surface.

As evening approached, Emily decided to set her net in the lake. It was dark by the time she and Donald got everything ready. Donald manoeuvred their small boat with his oars as Emily unravelled the net from the stern. From my small canoe I captured a few images with my camera. Despite pitch-black conditions and manual focus, I got lucky with some clear images. Like other Tŝilhqot'in women, Emily used the materials she had at hand to weave her gillnet out of number ten thread purchased from the general store.

The next morning Donald hauled in the catch.

One day Donald Ekks asked if I'd like to see a real pit house. "There's one still standing over by the Chilko River," he told me. "I'll show it to you." So we piled into my truck and Donald gave directions. Partway down the Chilko-Newton Road from Henry's Crossing to Redstone, he got me to turn left up a narrow bush track away from the river. This was the road Doris, Madeline and Cas Lulua, Emily's nieces and nephew, used to get to their Blue Creek winter feeding grounds for their cattle at the headwaters of Bidwell Creek. Just past a small lake, Donald got me to stop. A short trek through the bush along the lakeshore took us to a small opening in the forest canopy, where Donald paused. He pointed to the ruins of an underground structure with the timbers and earth-covered frame still very much intact. The building was square in shape, unlike the round pit house depressions usually found in the Cariboo Chilcotin and southern British Columbia. Donald said it had been built many years earlier by Emily's brother Felix for their grandfather Babstick. An earth lodge with its wooden infrastructure still in place was a rare find in the mid-1990s.

A few years later I was fighting a forest fire up the slope from the lake. During a break in the action I walked down to check on the status of Felix's pit house. To my delight it had survived the holocaust unscathed.

Emily Lulua Ekks sets her gillnet at night in Gwedzin Lake. Sage Birchwater photo

In June 1994 Emily's family decided to have a surprise eightieth birthday party for her at Gwedzin. It was a dual celebration actually, because she and her husband shared the same birthday. On June 11, Emily turned eighty and Donald turned seventy-one. By that time the couple had been together nearly forty years.

Just how the family intended to keep the celebration a secret is still a mystery. It took months of planning. People had to be notified well in advance; family members lived in diverse locations across the landscape, and many didn't have telephones.

A few days before the gathering, some members of the family arrived to construct a makeshift bandshell and stage. This included setting up a portable sound system covered with tarps in case of rain.

Donald Ekks stands by the underground house Emily's brother, Felix Lulua, built for their grandfather, Babstick, near Henry's Crossing. Sage Birchwater photo

Felix Lulua at Alex Mattheson's cabin near Gwedzin, around 1948. Alex Mattheson collection

·The only thing missing was Emily and Donald. No one seemed to know where they were. At the same time, they weren't too worried. They figured the couple would be back eventually. So preparations continued with the addition of outdoor kitchens and an extra outhouse or two. More people arrived, including the musicians from Xeni Gwet'in who had been booked in advance.

On the evening before the celebration, I ran into Emily and Donald at a funeral in Anahim Lake, 120 kilometres away. "Aren't you supposed to be at Gwedzin for the birthday party?" I asked.

"We catch a ride with a Forestry guy yesterday," Donald explained. "He picked us up hitchhiking. Maybe you drive us back to Gwedzin tomorrow?"

So it was all set then. Emily and Donald had their ticket home almost as if fate had planned it. I was heading there anyway because the family had asked me to cover it for the newspaper. So I got to bring the honoured guests to their unique family celebration. As we rolled in, Gwedzin was uncharacteristically teeming with people. Tents, camps and vehicles were everywhere. Just another day in the magical lives of Emily and Donald.

When we got there, family members said they had wondered where the old couple were. "We were a bit concerned but not worried," one person said. "We figured they might be at a funeral somewhere. Good thing it was Anahim Lake and not over in Nazko."

At the gathering Emily was given the microphone to say a few words. A family member translated for those who didn't speak Tŝilhqot'in.

"Gwedzin has always been Tŝilhqot'in country," she stated. "Even today it continues to be an important camping ground. Years ago people travelled to Tŝimol Ch'ed [the Potato Mountains] every spring by horse and wagon to harvest the *sunt'iny* [wild potatoes], and they would stop at Gwedzin. They made camp here, caught fish and rested up before going up the mountain to dig the *sunt'iny*. Then when they came back they stopped here again and caught fish before going back to Redstone."

At the end of June 2000, I was working up in Anahim Lake when a friend phoned from Tatla Lake to let me know that Emily Ekks had passed away. Apparently she had been bathing in Gwedzin Lake, preparing to head off to a funeral, and she keeled over on her way back to her cabin and died of a heart attack. That's where Donald found her in the tall grass.

A week or so later Emily's funeral was held at Gwedzin, and it was no small affair. People came from all over. After the ceremony Emily's casket was taken to the family burial grounds at Naghatalhchuẑ, and she was laid to rest there. Many people followed the procession over the dusty, rugged road to this unique setting where the peaks of Tŝil?oŝ and ?Eniyud were both clearly visible.

A Tŝilhqot'in legend captures the mystery of these peaks and explains why wild potatoes, known by botanists as spring beauty, are not found any farther west on the Chilcotin Plateau.

Tŝil?oŝ and his wife, ?Eniyud, were travelling across the land with their children, planting the wild potatoes. They got as far as Nemiah Valley, on the east side of Tŝilhqox Biny (Chilko Lake), where they split up. Tŝil?oŝ stayed in Nemiah Valley with three of their children while ?Eniyud and their other children continued farther west. After she got to the far side of Telhiqox (Tatlayoko Valley), ?Eniyud looked back. That's when fate played its unkind hand. Immediately ?Eniyud and Tŝil?oŝ, as well as their children, all turned into mountains: Tŝil?oŝ in Nemiah Valley above Xeni Biny (Konni Lake), and ?Eniyud on the west side of Telhiqox Biny (Tatlayoko Lake).

Former Xeni Gwet'in Chief Roger William takes the meaning of the legend a step further.

"To me Tŝil?oŝ is a leader who had a family and this family separated, and so he looks after the land and his people forever," he told me. "Tŝil?oŝ and ?Eniyud are protectors of the land, animals, fish, waters and Tŝilhqot'in tradition. If you'd been around to see Tŝil?oŝ and ?Eniyud before the Tŝilhqot'in War compared with today, it wouldn't look much different."

And people are cautioned to always show the utmost respect for these mountains. "Never point your finger at them" is one warning. And many non-Indigenous folks heed this advice.

REMEMBERING EMILY

Emily's family remembered her this way in a memorial booklet made for her funeral:

> ?Inkel (Mother), as she was fondly known, was the pillar of our family. She was a traditional person, living a life of simplicity in the heart of Tŝilhqot'in Territory. Up until the day she died, she was living where she liked to be at Gwedzin.
>
> This is where she lived in the summertime. This is the place she carried on the traditional activities of the Tŝilhqot'in People. Any time you came to visit her you would find her doing a number of things. Tanning deer or moose hides, sewing moccasins or gloves, drying deer or moose meat. One of her favourite activities was to set out gillnets on Cochin Lake. She set out the nets using a boat or a raft; usually it was a raft. She did this because this is what she had done for many years to feed her family during the long winter months. During late August and early September ?Inkel and Donald would move to Henry's Crossing and start getting ready to smoke and dry salmon. She always dried more than enough salmon to last all winter. One summer we counted three

hundred salmon while she was putting them in bags to store over the winter. At times Mom would ask her, 'You are too old to be doing so much work. Why do you need to dry so much salmon every year?' Her answer was, 'There are many grandkids and they will need dry salmon during the winter months.'

?Inkel was an oral historian for our family and for the Tŝilhqot'in People. She was our living encyclopedia of stories, customs and culture of the Tŝilhqot'in People. Any time we wanted to know things of importance, she was there to pass on her knowledge. Today the book of knowledge is forever closed, but we will not dwell on the loss. Instead we will cherish in her memory, the stories, customs and culture of the Tŝilhqot'in People she has handed down to us.

Joyce Charleyboy, Minnie Charleyboy's oldest daughter, wrote in Emily's memorial booklet that it is important to heed her grandmother's words.

"One of the things I vividly remember her saying at her eightieth birthday party was this: 'Don't keep going to places you don't belong. Doing that isn't good for you. Stay close to home and teach your children the proper way to live.'

People came from miles around for Emily Lulua Ekks's funeral at Gwedzin in June 2000. Left centre is Emily's sister Eliza Williams from Tŝideldel. In the centre foreground is Susan Sulin Cahoose from Fish Trap, near Nimpo Lake. Susan was the daughter of Sam and Mary Sulin, and she married Gus Cahoose from Ulkatcho. Emma Williams from Tŝideldel is standing at the right. After the service, Emily was taken to the family burial grounds at Naghatalhchuẑ. Sage Birchwater photo

Above: Memorial procession for Emily Lulua Ekks at Henry's Crossing, a year after her passing. Flag bearers Roger William, left, and Patrick Charleyboy, right, are joined by Ivor Myers, Kimberly William, Ubill Hunlin, Joyce Charleyboy, Marion William and Gilbert Solomon. Sage Birchwater photo

"To me she was saying we should always know where our home is. And we should raise our children to the best of our ability. We should also help people in any way we can. ?Inkel helped family and friends in any way she was able. Whether it was giving away dried salmon or meat, or giving away moccasins or gloves. When you visited her you never went away hungry and never left her place without taking something she had given you."

Emily was born at the north end of Tsuniah Lake in 1914 to Jack Lulua and Jennie Nemiah. She was raised by the Chief of Nemiah Valley, Seal Canim, and his wife, also named Jennie, after her mother died when she was only two years old.

Emily had four sisters and four brothers and had eight children of her own—Minnie, Ubill, Ellen, Lilly, Donald, Oggie, Raymond and David—and two grandsons, Patrick and Jim, she also raised.

Joyce said Emily raised these children in times when there was no welfare, family allowance or any type of assistance, and she raised them in the traditional manner, hunting, fishing and gathering. "My mom and her siblings would tell ?Inkel she shouldn't just take off and hitchhike. But my grandmother had her own way of doing things. She was a free spirit and whenever she had the urge to travel, she and Donald would set off on foot and catch a ride with whoever would pick them up."

Celebrating ?Inkel Emily Lulua Ekks's eightieth birthday are Emily's daughter Minnie Charleyboy and Minnie's granddaughter Charm Cooper, dancing to the music of Xeni Gwet'in musicians. Sage Birchwater photo

A year after Emily's passing, in June 2001, a special ceremony was held at the Brittany gathering site at Henry's Crossing to honour her. Roger William, then Chief of Xeni Gwet'in, unveiled a plaque in Emily's name to recognize the person who had caught the biggest fish at the annual Brittany gathering.

James "Jim" Lulua Sr. and his wife, Dinah, run a few head of cattle in Nemiah Valley, and at sixty-nine, Jim still drives the local school bus. He and his brother Patrick were adopted by their grandmother Emily when their mother, Ellen Lulua, died at Alexis Creek when Jim was only three or four years old.

"I was at Anaham [Tl'etinqox] Hospital with Mom on her deathbed," Jim told me. "I was being taken care of by a nun. She took me out to Lee's Corner. I was four years old and I didn't know my mom had passed."

His mother was buried at Tl'etinqox, and he's still not sure where her grave is located. He was brought back home to Henry's Crossing and Naghatalhchuẑ country, where his aunts Minnie Charleyboy and Lilly Lulua looked after him until he was old enough to go to residential school. He said the whole family pitched in and took care of him and Patrick. "Lilly's son Roy and I were more or less like brothers."

Jim fondly remembers his grandparents' annual trip to the Anahim Lake Stampede.

Above: Since Emily's death in 2000, her Gwedzin cabin, built by David and James Lulua in the 1960s, has stood abandoned. Sage Birchwater photo

Below: Cousins William and Oggie Lulua share a few stories at Emily's memorial gathering a year after her passing. Sage Birchwater photo

"We'd head out the first weekend in July with their team and horses, four days before the rodeo starts. We'd get to Anahim Lake on the Thursday afternoon. Coming back from the rodeo Donald Ekks might find a job for a few days. Then we'd get ready for our Potato Mountain trip. We'd head down to Tatlayoko and my uncles would shoe our horses with special shoes for climbing the mountain. We'd spend three weeks in July camping up there. I spent a lot of time with my grandma picking potatoes all day long. When the sun went down, we went home back to camp."

When they were finished digging the potatoes, the work still wasn't done.

"We had to clean all the potatoes," Jim said. "Then we took a thread and needle and made a necklace out of them. We dried them that way."

Jim was just a baby when he first went up the Potato Mountains.

"My grandma's niece Madeline [Lulua] said she packed me around up there," he said.

When Jim was fifteen years old he no longer had to go back to Saint Joseph's Mission residential school, and he spent more time with Emily.

"Grandma spent time in places here and there utilizing all the territory. She had her place near Tatla Lake, and her camp at Gwedzin. She'd go down the river five or six miles from Henry's Crossing and she had another cabin. Lilly had a cabin there too beside the river. Roy Lulua and I went all the way to Tatlayoko with a team and wagon to get lumber to put a roof on Lilly's house. Our uncle Ubill Lulua worked at the Lignum sawmill there. I was fifteen or sixteen when we did that. I remember Grandma's cabin by the river, packing sacks and sacks of moss to do the chinking."

Jim worked with his uncles to build the little cabin for Emily and Donald at Gwedzin. His uncle Oggie Lulua started the first four or five rounds, and then Jim and David Lulua took over. Jim is a couple of years older than David.

"We were camped out at the end of October," Jim recalled. "Grandma told us it's going to get cold soon so we better hurry up and get the ridgepoles up. We finished the log work, then got the roof put on in the first week of November and there was already snow on the ground. We were still camped out and it was pretty cold."

He said the roof was quite low, but in that country, when you have to heat a cabin with firewood, that's not a bad thing.

"I had to learn not to hit my head on the ceiling, but it was good to get the roof logs in place. Finally we got the roofing paper on."

After he was free from residential school, Jim said, Emily taught him how to trap during the winter.

"We moved around as a big family. In springtime, as soon as it was warm enough to be out of the house, we'd camp out."

He spent winters at his grandmother's cabin at Gwedzin or at the River Cabin beside the Chilko River, trapping lynx and squirrels.

Donald and Emily are surrounded by family during their birthday celebration in 1994. Left to right are David Lulua, Ronnie Solomon (at the microphone behind), Gerald Royce William, James Lulua Sr. and Oggie Lulua. Sage Birchwater photo

Group shot of family and friends celebrating the birthdays of Emily Lulua Ekks and Donald Ekks at Gwedzin in June 1994. Sage Birchwater photo

"I did a lot of walking. I'd go from the River Cabin to Blue Creek where my uncle Casimil and aunts Doris and Madeline fed their cattle in the winter at the head of Bidwell Creek. When I think of it now, that was a long ways to walk."

When he was around fifteen, Jim and Roy Lulua spent a winter feeding cattle for Alf and Gerry Bracewell at Skinner Meadow.

"It was so cold we had to bring the harness right inside the house. It was thirty below so it didn't take long for the harness to get stiff again once we put it on the horses. We'd go up and chop a hole in the ice for the cows to drink before getting the hay. When we got back with the hay we'd have to chop it open again. We'd make a fire every now and then, and chop the ice some more."

Jim spent a summer cowboying for C1 Ranch of Alexis Creek, which ranged its cattle around Eagle Lake.

"October was roundup time," he said. "Once we gathered them up we chased the cows down the River Road. There were others waiting at Bidwell Creek to chase them to Alexis Creek."

Jim said he was seventeen when he last did that.

"Then I hung around town like a Trooper for a couple of years. The late Marvin [Baptiste] looked me up all the time. He was Chief back then. 'Why don't you come home with us?' he'd always ask. Finally he convinced me to come out of town. I was nineteen or twenty when

Marvin brought me out to Nemiah to live with him, and I've been here ever since."

Jim's uncle Donald Lulua was part of the Trooper crowd in Williams Lake when Jim was there. Then after Jim moved back home, he'd see Donald occasionally out west.

"Donald came and went. He'd spend time with us at home, then he'd take off and go back to town again."

DONALD LULUA'S PASSING

Donald Lulua, who introduced me to his family back in 1977, was only fifty years old when he passed away in 1988. A big funeral was held for him at Tŝideldel. Father John Brioux, an Oblate priest, said Donald was the first member of the Tŝideldel community to reach out to him.

"He had a peace about him which spoke to me and touched me," Father John told me. "He had an attitude of openness and friendliness."

That's how I remember Donald too. An ambassador of his people. Someone who reached out to you and made you feel welcome.

What made Emily Lulua Ekks special was that she was vital right to the end. She died with her boots on, as the expression goes, fully engaged in her life's purpose and activity. Of course in Emily's case, she was wearing moccasins.

I'm sure that from Emily's perspective, her passing was more like a momentary pause in her busy life before moving on to the next phase of her journey. For those of us left behind, it was more like the passing of an era.

A drawing of Emily Lulua Ekks by Yunesit'in artist Fred Brigham.

The Haynes Family of Tatlayoko

Harry and Fran Haynes

For more than two decades in the 1980s and '90s, Harry and Fran Haynes were the heart and soul of Tatlayoko Valley. Their CB (citizens' band) radio handle was "Coffee House," and for many years they ran the post office out of their home. It was routine for most people in the valley to drop in and visit when they picked up their mail, and many of us who got our mail at Tatla Lake just stopped by to visit.

The Hayneses' coffee pot was always on, and Fran dutifully kept her cookie jar full. Harry of course had endless stories to tell, and some of them were true. My indoctrination as a writer of local history likely began in their kitchen.

There was no residential phone service in Tatlayoko Valley until the late 1980s, but there were two public radio pay phones along the forty-kilometre stretch between Tatla Lake and Tatlayoko. The first phone booth stood by itself beside the road at the junction of McGhee Road and the old road to Little Eagle Lake. It seemed so strange standing there in the middle of nowhere that we gave it the nickname Surrealistic Phone Booth.

The second public pay phone was in a more settled part of the valley in front of Harry and Fran's place. As a courtesy the telephone company hooked up an extension line from the phone booth into the Haynes residence. This allowed Harry and Fran to answer the phone whenever it rang and take messages for everyone in the valley. Then they'd contact people over the CB radio or leave notes in the appropriate mail slot. When you came to make your call, you could stand outside in the phone booth or go inside Harry and Fran's house if the weather was cold. Their welcome mat was always extended.

Harry and Fran became surrogate parents to a community of young people who found their way into Tatlayoko Valley during the 1970s and '80s and ended up staying. These were the idealistic back-to-the-land days when young people from the cities were seeking a lifestyle in rural parts of North America. Later, Harry and Fran became surrogate grandparents for the offspring of these latter-day settlers.

Harry was sixteen when he arrived in the Chilcotin two days before Christmas of 1929. Earlier that year his mother, Del Naomi Haynes, had been working as a cook at the Church Ranch in Big Creek, and she learned that Bill Christie, a Chilcotin old-timer, was looking for someone to help him with his ranch chores at Alexis Lakes. She told Harry when she got home to New Westminster, and he seized on the idea and made arrangements with Bill to come up and work for him.

Fran and Harry Haynes of Tatlayoko in the 1980s. Photo from *Hoofprints in History*, Vol. 4, page 33

Harry took the steamship from Vancouver to Squamish and jumped on the Pacific Great Eastern passenger train to Williams Lake. When he arrived in town he went to the Lakeview Hotel across the street from the railway station, hoping to find a ride to the Chilcotin.

"I went into the hotel and asked if there was any way I could get to Alexis Creek, and they told me Alex Graham was staying in the hotel and would be heading home the next day," Harry told me.

Alex Graham, a rancher from Alexis Creek, had a big old McLaughlin-Buick touring car with a canvas roof but no sides on it, and he invited Harry to ride back with him. It was a bit chilly for winter travel, but Harry was more concerned about his safety because of Alex's erratic driving.

"He drove all over the road, zigzagging and spinning this way and that," Harry said.

Fortunately they made it to the Grahams' ranch house in Alexis Creek in one piece, and Harry spent the night there. The next day Jess Morton, a rancher from Alexis Lakes, showed up with a team and buggy to pick up the Christmas mail, and he gave

"Surrealistic Phone Booth" at the junction of McGhee Road and Tatlayoko Road. Junah Birchwater photo

Harry a lift to his Spain Lake ranch. Bill Christie lived another day's travel beyond there in the Franklin Meadow country. Jess Morton had picked up Bill Christie's mail as well. The next day was Christmas, and Jess brought the mail and Harry over the mountain to Bill Christie's. That's how Harry's life in the Chilcotin began.

"It was fifteen or twenty miles from Jess Morton's ranch to Bill Christie's, and Jess stayed overnight with old Bill and went back home the next day on Boxing Day," Harry said.

He marvelled at the ingenious strategies people in the Chilcotin used to survive. To stay warm while travelling in sub-zero temperatures, Jess put a couple of salt blocks into the cookstove oven and got them really hot. Then he wrapped them in blankets and put them on the floor of the buggy to keep his feet warm. Harry noted, "Those salt blocks would stay hot all day long wrapped in blankets."

Harry said his feet were warm but the rest of him was freezing.

"I wasn't dressed for a Chilcotin winter. I didn't know enough to put on lots of clothes, so I did quite a bit of jumping off and running to stay warm."

He stayed with Bill Christie for eight years.

"I didn't really have a job. The old man advertised in the Williams Lake newspaper for a companion. He gave me enough money for tobacco."

Harry made more money trapping than working for wages, he said. Of course, nobody in the Chilcotin had any money during the Great Depression to pay for help.

In the spring of 1930 Del Naomi Haynes headed back to the Chilcotin, this time for good. Her sister Daisy Dack from Victoria drove her and her four younger boys—Lou, Ray, Laurie and Ken—to Tatlayoko Valley from New Westminster in her old Hudson-Essex car so Del could run the post office for pioneer rancher K.B. (Kennon Beverly) Moore at the Circle X Ranch. Lou turned fifteen that year, Ray twelve, Laurie ten and Ken seven.

In those days mail was delivered every two weeks to Tatlayoko by Tommy Hodgson, who had the weekly mail contract from Williams Lake to the Chilcotin. He'd alternate taking the mail to Anahim Lake one week, then to Tatlayoko the next.

"When we first came to the Chilcotin my brothers and I just coyoted around," Harry told me. "The way we made a living was just travelling around. We had a pack horse and a saddle horse and we'd just head out. We just rode all over the country looking for jobs. Any kind of job at all, it didn't matter how much it paid, as long as they would feed us."

Harry and his brother Lou worked for Tommy Lulua, a Tŝilhqot'in man who had a small ranch a dozen kilometres from Tatlayoko Valley at the west end of Big Eagle (Choelquoit) Lake. Tommy hired them to dig a

ditch to lower the water level in a lake. After two weeks they were paid with a horse for their troubles, and that became Lou's horse. Then they worked a month for Scotty Shields, a recent arrival from Scotland living in Tatlayoko, and got another horse. "That was my horse," Harry said.

The following summer Lou took his horse to Jess Morton's place at Alexis Lakes, and Jess harnessed it with another horse

The five Haynes brothers. Left to right: Ken, Laurie, Ray, Lou and Harry. Photo courtesy Harry Haynes

Young Billyboy rode his Thoroughbred horse at a full gallop for forty kilometres from Alexis Lakes to Alexis Creek to get a doctor after rancher Jess Morton lost his arm in a mowing machine accident. Photo courtesy Euphrasia Williams

Lou Haynes, far left, and Harry Haynes, far right, are joined by two other cowboys as they made their way through the Chilcotin in the 1930s and '40s, working at odd jobs throughout the country. Photo courtesy Harry Haynes

to cut hay. Somehow the bridle got hooked and the team ran away. Jess got bucked off in front of the mower and got run over by the cutting bar. "He lost one arm and all those teeth dug into his body," Harry said. "He had numerous wounds all up and down his sides. A Tŝilhqot'in man from Tl'etinqox, Young Billyboy, saved his life."

Young Billyboy acted quickly, racing over to the house to alert Jess's brother, Bert. They got a sack of flour and stuck the stump of Jess's severed arm right into the sack of flour and tied the sack around it.

"That's what saved Jess's life," Harry said. "He would have bled to death otherwise."

Then Young Billyboy jumped on his Thoroughbred racehorse and rode flat out for nearly forty kilometres to Alexis Creek to get the doctor.

"He made it in about an hour and a quarter and his horse damn near died," Harry said.

Young Billyboy found Doc Hallows, who jumped in his car and sped up to Alexis Lakes. He got there within two hours of Young Billyboy heading out on his heroic horseback ride. Doc Hallows treated the injuries, and he said the flour did indeed save Jess Morton's life.

After Jess recovered from his injuries he was forced to quit ranching and moved to Williams Lake, where he became the gardener for the courthouse. When he reached old age, Jess and Bert Morton shared a house in Glendale, a subdivision of Williams Lake along the Soda Creek Road just outside of town. Harry said he spotted Jess one day "all crippled up" with arthritis, walking down the street with an old black dog.

"The funny thing, Jess said the old black dog wasn't his dog at all," Harry said. "Every morning when the old man headed out for his walk, the dog was there. They were both old and they'd go down a mile or two and come back. Jess said he never sees the dog again until the next morning. 'He's just an old bastard like me,' Jess told me. 'I don't know where he comes from.'"

Harry remembered visits from the Oblate priest Father Francois Marie Thomas during his time working for Bill Christie.

"At Christmastime Father Thomas used to go through the whole country and hold Mass. He went up to Quesnel first, then over to Nazko. From Nazko he'd go to Chezacut, then over to Redbrush and Redstone, before heading back to Saint Joseph's Mission in Williams Lake."

Harry said Father Thomas would stop at Bill Christie's on his way from Nazko to Chezacut.

"We were about halfway so he used to stay overnight with us all the time."

He remembered one time Father Thomas came through on a Friday.

"He had a Native man driving the sleigh for him. When he got there he asked old Bill Christie what he was having for supper. Bill said he had some beef cooking and Father Thomas said, 'You know I can't eat beef on Friday.' Then Father Thomas said he had some fish out in his sled, and he went out and reached under the canvas tarp and pulled out a beaver tail the Natives at Nazko had given him. That's what he had for dinner. We ate beef and Father Thomas ate beaver tail … and he called it 'fish.'"

After several years riding with his brothers, Harry moved to Tatlayoko Valley. He took up land at the mouth of Lincoln Creek and stayed there for good. His mother, Del Naomi Haynes, moved in with him during the last two decades of her life.

LAURIE HAYNES

Laurie Haynes was nine years old when he arrived in Tatlayoko from New Westminster in the spring of 1930 with his mother, Del Naomi Haynes, and three of his brothers, Lou, Ray and Ken.

Del had separated from her union activist husband, John Kemp Haynes, because he was unable to get a job to support his family. His continual standing up for workers' rights got him blacklisted so employers refused to hire him.

With five children to feed, Del was looking for a new start when she took the job offer from K.B. Moore to run the Tatlayoko post office.

"At nine years old I didn't know too much what was going on," Laurie told me. "Just roll with the punches. We adapted to the life in the valley pretty quick. It didn't take us long to fit in. Within a year we could all ride horses."

The Haynes brothers in New Westminster in the late 1920s, a couple of years before they left for the Chilcotin with their mother, Del Naomi Haynes, in 1930. Left to right are Laurie, Ray, Ken (at the bottom), Lou and Harry. Photo courtesy Harry Haynes

Emery Bellamy, a neighbour who had moved to Tatlayoko Valley from Montana six years earlier, gifted the Haynes family with an old white mare named Belle. A few years later Scotty Shields gave Laurie his first horse, a small stud he managed to cut out of the wild bunch on the Eagle Lake sidehill.

"I'll never forget," Laurie said. "Scotty rode into our place to get the mail one day, leading this little black horse. He got out of the saddle and handed me the lead rope, and said, 'Laurie, I brought you a horse.' It was a little black shitter stud [a colloquial name for a horse that consumed hay all winter and converted it all to manure]. He had castrated it, broke it to lead and brought it over. It was the gentlest little cayuse you ever saw in your life." Laurie named it Scotty.

James "Scotty" Shields had come to the country only a few years earlier from Scotland and eventually married Margaret Bellamy, daughter of Emery and Alice Bellamy. Laurie remembered driving over from Tatlayoko to Big Creek for Dick and Rona Church's wedding in August 1931. (The Church family were pioneers at Big Creek, where Dick's father, H.E. Church, homesteaded in 1903.) Scotty was driving Laurie's aunt's Hudson-Essex, the car in which they had arrived from New Westminster the year before, and Scotty and Del sang the whole way.

"Scotty could sing like a bird and Mom had a tremendous voice," Laurie said. "They knew every song there was."

Laurie spent several Christmases with Leonard and Hilda Butler, who had settled in the West Branch Valley of the Homathko at Bluff Lake in the late 1920s.

James "Scotty" Shields. Photo from *Hoofprints in History*, Vol. 3, page 36

In the Dirty Thirties there was no money to buy presents, so people made all their own gifts.

"Leonard Butler made all the presents he gave his family," Laurie recalled. "A spinning wheel for his mother, Ada Holt; a set of chairs for his wife, Hilda; a wooden tricycle for his son, Lee; and a set of handmade snowshoes for me. Of course Christmas Day was like any other day in ranching country. You got up and fed cows. But it was festive."

Established families like the Bellamys, McGhees, Purjues, Moores and Butlers had big Christmas dinners and invited the loners and bachelors from around the neighbourhood to join them. Laurie said turkey was never on the menu in the early years because nobody had a fridge or deep-freeze, but there was plenty of the "King's beef"

Leonard Butler. Photo by Frank Swannell, 1927. BC Archives I-59517 courtesy the Royal BC Museum and Archives

or wild game available. K.B. Moore had an ice house, but it wasn't adequate to preserve a bird the size of a turkey indefinitely.

"You didn't just go into Williams Lake and buy a bunch of groceries and a turkey like you do today," Laurie explained. "You went in with the beef drive in the fall, and when you came back out, that was it. Bringing perishables out on the mail truck from Williams Lake was out of the question too, because it was unreliable. It could take anywhere from two to ten days depending on the weather and the road conditions. You sure couldn't set any dates on the mail arriving. You get that big rain in the fall and holy smokes. As it was, mail delivery to Tatlayoko Valley was only every second week."

Laurie said the roads west of Alexis Creek just weren't roads.

"It's hard to realize just how tough the roads were unless you were there."

He described a near miss he had on the main Chilcotin Highway when he was on medical leave from the army during the Second World War. "I came home on sick leave while recovering from a hernia operation. I took the train from Squamish and met Percy Hance and E.P. [Ed Penrose] Lee in Williams Lake. They had been in town for a week on a big drunk.

We headed out in E.P. Lee's old truck, and when we got to the edge of town, E.P. Lee got out of the truck and said, 'You're driving.' Well, I was in no shape to be driving. I'd just had an operation the week before."

Nevertheless Laurie took the wheel and drove from the Borland Ranch in Williams Lake to Hanceville, where Percy Hance got out. Then he continued driving west to Tommy Lee's store in Alexis Creek. On their way across Anaham Flats between Hanceville and Alexis Creek, they encountered Frank Mayfield of Chilco Ranch coming the opposite way on the wrong side of the road.

"I was in the left-hand lane and he was in the right-hand lane," Laurie recalled. "We were both on the wrong side of the road. But there was no way we could change lanes because we were both in deep ruts and couldn't get out. So we just passed each other on the wrong side of the road and just kept going. Old E.P. missed the whole thing because he was snoring."

Laurie dropped E.P. Lee at Tommy Lee's store and went off to bunk with Tom and Gertrude Harvey to wait for the mail stage that was due in three days.

"I always stayed with the Harveys. I'd done a lot of work for old Tom Harvey in the early years. I'd babysit their place when they came out to Chilko Lake to look after salmon in the fall. Tom Harvey was hired by the Pacific Salmon Authority to monitor the Chilko sockeye run."

The first year Laurie arrived in Tatlayoko, he and his brothers attended school in K.B. Moore's house. The arrival of three school-aged Haynes kids helped tip the scales so there were enough children for the community to be eligible for a school. The parents of the children chipped in and built a new one-room school, and Laurie and his brothers were conscripted to help out.

Gladys Royce was the teacher, and later she married Cecil Bellamy. A few years later the demographics of school-aged kids shifted to the north end of the valley, so the school building was hauled up there next to the Bellamy Ranch on Crazy Creek.

With his mother running the Tatlayoko post office, Laurie grew up getting to know people from across the region who came to get their mail. The large extended Lulua family was part of a strong Tŝilhqot'in

Tatlayoko School, built in 1931 by the parents of the school's first students. Photo from *Hoofprints in History*, Vol. 8, page 45

community that still retained their old ways and their connection to the land. They also adapted to some settler traditions like ranching.

"Tommy Lulua had twenty-five or thirty head of cattle, and every fall when the beef drive went from Tatlayoko across the Eagle Lake sidehill, he'd always put four or five head in the drive to Williams Lake," Laurie said.

The Lulua clan occupied the country around Big Eagle Lake and the upper Chilko River, all the way over to Tsuniah Lake. Jack Lulua, patriarch of the family, made a big impression on Laurie, who described him as a happy-go-lucky guy who didn't care what other people thought of him. "The Tŝilhqot'in people that I met weren't impressed with strangers. They didn't give a damn if you had a Lincoln Continental and ten million dollars in the bank; you didn't have the freedom they had."

He said Jack Lulua used to walk down the trail leading his pack horse and singing at the top of his lungs. "That's why people used to call him Crazy Jack, but he was a long way from crazy. He was an individual. He went his own way, did his own thing, and if you didn't like it, well, that was just too bad for you. Over in Chezacut one time Jack Lulua was working in the hayfield for Charlie and Martha Mulvahill. During their lunch break Mrs. Mulvahill came in and asked Jack if he was really crazy. He looked around and said, 'Nighttime maybe a little bit crazy. Daytime I be all right.'"

Laurie remembered a time when Jack Lulua was camped out with his family on Sunflower Hill, partway up the trail to the Potato Mountains. Laurie and two of his brothers stopped to visit, and Jack told the whole story of the Chilcotin War.

"He said he went with War Chief Lhatŝ'aŝ?in when they massacred Waddington's road-building party down in the canyon. He said he was a young boy then, maybe twelve or thirteen years old. He told the whole story, how they waited until the road crew went to work, then killed the cook and the flunky. Then they killed the guys on top of the canyon tending the ropes. Then cut all the ropes and pulled all the poles off the pins so the guys out there couldn't get back. Then they dropped rocks on them until they killed them all.

Tommy Lulua with grandson Edmond Lulua in front of his cabin at Henry's Crossing. Photo courtesy the Henry Lulua family

Old Jack Lulua told the whole story. My brothers Lou and Ray were there too. We were just kids. The old grease trail went down the east side of Tatlayoko Lake to the coast. The Tŝilhqot'ins would take dried deer meat down and bring eulachon oil back."

LOU HAYNES

Lou Haynes was fifteen years old when he came to Tatlayoko Valley. By 1932 his mother, Del Naomi Haynes, had taken over the Tatlayoko post office from K.B. Moore and had the post office in her house. Lou was assistant postmaster. With his parents separated and his dad, John Kemp Haynes, still in the Lower Mainland, Lou found a father figure and mentor in Scotty Shields, who lived up the valley a piece. They remained lifelong friends.

"Scotty gave me my first horse," Lou told me. "He got it from the wild bunch at Eagle Lake."

When Lou was nineteen years old he rode his horse to Tommy Walker's stampede at Stuie. It was 1934, and it was 160 kilometres from Tatlayoko to the Atnarko River in the Bella Coola Valley. But in those days distances were of small consequence when it came to a social event.

"A whole bunch of us went down from Tatla Lake," Lou said. "Tommy Walker had Stuie Lodge at the time, and he held one of the first stampedes we ever had in this country."

One of the riders who went from Tatla Lake was Ollie Nukalow, also known as Johnny Robertson. Ollie was a strong, capable man about ten years older than Lou who worked at the Graham Ranch in Tatla Lake. Lou said Ollie showed him how to catch fish in the Dean River.

"On our way back from the Stuie Stampede we stopped at Natsadalia, where the Dean River flows out of Anahim Lake and goes down to Abuntlet Lake. Natsadalia Crossing is always good fishing right there. Ollie showed me how to catch rainbow trout with a piece of string and a hook tied to a willow stick."

Lou Haynes grew up in Tatlayoko Valley and worked at many jobs riding across the Chilcotin. Sage Birchwater photo

Ollie's mother was Loozap, a Tŝilhqot'in woman from Redstone. His father was Jim Robertson, a Scottish immigrant who had settled in

Chiwid, also known as Lilly Skinner Jack, was a Tŝilhqot'in recluse who lived outside in the Chilcotin for more than half a century. Veera Bonner photo

Nemiah Valley. Jim died tragically of a gunshot wound when Ollie was a boy. Some said it was self-inflicted, but others insisted it was murder.

Ollie's older half-sister was Chiwid (Lilly Skinner Jack), who later became famous as the invincible recluse who lived outside in the wilds of the Chilcotin for fifty years. They had the same mother but different dads. Chiwid's father was Charlie Skinner, an American who pre-empted a big meadow in the Eagle Lake country between Tatlayoko Valley and Naghatalhchuẑ, or Big Eagle Lake. It is still known as Skinner Meadow today.

On the strength of a railway survey from Bute Inlet up the Homathko River to the interior of British Columbia in the mid-1880s, Charlie Skinner decided to build a stopping house on the proposed route. He and Frank Render, a master log builder from Kleena Kleene, went in together on the project. The dovetail corners of the building are so precise you'd be hard pressed to fit a piece of paper between the joinery of the logs. The half-constructed building is still standing. The walls of the structure are nearly 2.5 metres tall, but the roof was never added. The word is that Charlie Skinner and Frank Render had an argument over a jar of jam, and the project was abandoned.

Perhaps another explanation for the unfinished edifice was the decision not to build a railway to Bute Inlet. Once it was decided to build the Grand Trunk Pacific Railway to Prince Rupert, completed in 1914, Canada had its second cross-country rail link to the Pacific Ocean, and all other rail line proposals to the coast were cancelled. At any rate the unfinished Skinner Meadow roadhouse stands as a testament to an earlier time. A copse of mature aspen trees has taken root and flourishes inside the log enclosure, measuring the time since work on the project ceased more than a century ago.

Lou Haynes said Charlie Skinner's real claim to fame, apart from siring Chiwid, was his role in overpopulating the Chilcotin with wild horses. He was a horse breeder who brought highly bred Clydesdale and Thoroughbred stallions into the country from Washington State to improve the quality of his herd. Then he simply turned the animals loose on the range to run with the wild bunch.

"The number of horses just built up and built up," Lou said. "Then as Charlie got older, the horses became unruly because he couldn't manage them.

Frank Render, who lived at Lillie Lake near Nimpo Lake, was a renowned axeman and log builder. His dovetail corner notches were so tight that it was impossible to fit a playing card between the logs. Photo from Joy Graham collection

The horses bred like wildfire. Pretty soon the whole country was full of wild horses."

There's an old story of Charlie Skinner being camped on the side of the road with a nice team of horses hooked up to his wagon, when a man he didn't recognize came along and started admiring the animals. When the man commented what a fine team of horses they were, Charlie responded, "Yep, and I got forty more just like them." Little did Charlie know he was talking to the tax assessor, and the stranger immediately jotted down the numbers. After that, Forestry wanted him to pay range fees on forty head, which Charlie refused to do. So Forestry said they were going to shoot them off. That's how it all got started.

The government wanted to reduce the number of wild horses in the Chilcotin to open up the country for cattle, Lou explained.

"By 1930 the range was eaten right down because these horses were on it winter and summer. Eagle Lake Henry and Bill Bliss offered to round up Charlie Skinner's horses for him so he could sell them, but Charlie refused. He didn't want anybody touching his horses. Eventually the Forest Service hired Scotty Shields and Jimmy Adams to start shooting horses. They killed over a thousand head the first year. You'd turn in the ears and get a dollar apiece for them."

Lou said the last big hunt was in 1939 when he and his brother Ray Haynes were hired by Forestry to shoot them.

"We started from Alexis Creek and went down to Big Creek, then worked our way west across Nemiah Valley to Tatla Lake. We got four hundred head of horses that winter."

He said the Forest Service paid them a wage of eighty dollars a month, plus they still got a dollar for each set of ears and five dollars for a set of ears and testicles.

"We had to keep a daily diary. We'd go out and shoot and cut all the ears off, and we'd also cut all the tails and manes. The war had just broken out, and we made more money on horsehair than from the wages and what we got for the ears. We sold it to the army. They wanted it for stuffing in the seats of vehicles and airplanes."

Lou described how they headed out with a sleigh and six head of horses. "Two were broke to harness, and you could ride them as well. We had a load of hay on the sleigh, and we'd just move and camp, move and camp. We'd fill sacks with the horsehair and ears and load them on the sleigh."

By spring they were at Skinner Meadow and the snow was melting.

"So we rode down home to Tatlayoko where we had an old Model T Ford made into a wagon and used the wagon for the last little while. Our last hunt was at Bidwell Creek."

Lou said he spent a couple of winters feeding cattle for Duke Martin, owner of the C1 Ranch at Alexis Creek.

"Duke Martin was running a thousand head of cattle, and in the wintertime he'd break the herd up and send them out to various meadows toward Nazko. I spent two winters out there on my own wintering five hundred head of cattle."

Besides forking sleigh load after sleigh load of loose hay from the big haystacks and feeding it out, Lou had to chop water holes for the cattle and set out the salt. On top of that, he had all the household chores of cooking and getting firewood to stay warm.

"I had a team of horses, a sleigh and a saddle horse, and I fed about six loads of hay a day," he said.

At the end of the day he'd bring a sleigh load of hay into the barnyard to feed his horses and the "hospital bunch."

"These were the cows that weren't doing too well, so you'd bring them into the barnyard and feed them a little extra," Lou explained.

Lou said it was a busy life. In the morning after breakfast, he'd get his horses harnessed and lined up, feed the few cows in the barnyard, then head out to the stackyard and start forking hay.

"Six loads of hay in one day. You forked it on and forked it off. If you had a few minutes to spare, you might shoot a moose and drag it in, or drag in a stick or two of firewood so you could saw it up at night."

A lot of people asked if he ever got lonesome working out there by himself.

"Heck, we didn't have time to get lonesome," he said. "When you got done with the chores, you were ready to go to bed. You got paid fifteen dollars a month along with your board."

From C1 Ranch, Lou went to work for Frank Mayfield at Chilco Ranch.

"All I did there was ride. Cowboy, and look after the cattle."

Chilco had a lot of good winter pastures where the cattle didn't have to be fed a lot of hay, he said.

"That's what made the big ranches what they were. Steep sidehills above the river stay bare of snow, and the cattle can rustle all winter."

But these ideal circumstances came with a price.

"When the weather gets bad and it gets icy, the cattle can slide off the hillside. Lots of cowboys got broken legs and ankles over that. Even if your horses are sharp-shoed, they can slip."

When a cow went over the hillside, Lou said, he had to go down and wrestle it back up top again.

"If it had a broken leg, you had to butcher it and drag the meat out. A cowboy would walk a mile to get a horse to ride a hundred yards."

DEL NAOMI HAYNES

Bev Butler was visiting her aunt Del Naomi Haynes in Tatlayoko Valley in the mid-1950s when she was awakened early one morning by a loud clatter in the kitchen. Along with the banging of pots and pans, she heard an unfamiliar voice: a man cursing up a blue streak.

"I was about fifteen or sixteen years old," Bev told me. "It was very early in the morning. About five o'clock. I don't know where Auntie Del and Harry had gone."

Bev said her eyes were like saucers as she stumbled out of bed and into the kitchen to find a Tŝilhqot'in man she had

Del Naomi Haynes moved to Tatlayoko Valley from New Westminster in 1930 to start a new life as postmaster. Bev Butler collection

never met before trying to light a fire in the cookstove.

"I guess the firewood was wet, and he was slamming stove lids and the tea kettle. I asked him who he was and he told me, 'Tommy Lulua.'"

Bev quickly found out that the door to the Haynes household was always open to Tommy Lulua. He was a neighbour who lived fifteen kilometres up the trail toward the Chilko River on the west end of Big Eagle Lake.

"He was allowed to come in any time of the day or night he wanted to. He took care of Auntie Del for years. He brought her deer meat, moose meat, fish, whatever he had. She'd give him vegetables out of her garden and helped him fill out his Timothy Eaton mail orders at the post office."

By the 1950s Del Haynes's four younger sons had left home and got their own places, but Harry had moved back to the valley, so she lived with him on Harry's pre-emption at the mouth of Lincoln Creek. Her youngest son, Ken, lived a short distance up the valley with his wife, Mary, and their children.

Billy Berwin, Del Naomi Haynes, unknown child and Harry Haynes in the Tatlayoko Valley during the 1950s. Bev Butler collection

Bev was the foster daughter of Del Haynes's sister Daisy Dack, a schoolteacher in Victoria. It was Daisy who brought Del and her four youngest sons to Tatlayoko from New Westminster in 1930 in her Hudson-Essex car. Bev was ten years old when she became Daisy Dack's foster daughter. She'd had a rough life, bouncing from foster home to foster home, until Daisy welcomed her and her younger sister Maureen into her household.

Bev met Del Haynes for the first time when Daisy brought the two girls up to Coombs on Vancouver Island, where Del was working as a housekeeper for an elderly man, Edward Berwin. The old man had in his care his young grandson Billy Berwin, about the same age as Bev and Maureen.

"They lived up at Coombs way back in the bush," Bev said. "We went to visit a couple of summers when we were ten or eleven. We thought it was the most wonderful place with apple trees and quince trees and goats all over the place."

The three youngsters would thumb rides to Qualicum Beach and spend all day swimming, Bev recalled.

"The tide would go way, way out. Then you'd have to swim like mad when the tide came in." Meanwhile Daisy Dack and Del Haynes would visit all day while the kids played.

"Billy took us up to the lookout and we'd play hide and seek and cowboys and Indians until dark."

Billy was eleven when Del Haynes brought him out to Tatlayoko Valley for the first time. It was Easter, and Billy rode in the back of the mail truck while Del sat beside the driver in the front seat. By summer Billy had decided he wanted to stay in Tatlayoko with Nanny Del.

Bev Butler went up to Tatlayoko for the first time in 1954.

"I was fourteen when Momma Dack drove us up in her little Morris Minor car to visit Auntie Del, and I fell in love with the Chilcotin."

She decided to come out again on her own the following year when she was fifteen.

"I worked picking strawberries to make enough money to come up to Williams Lake on the bus to visit Auntie Del."

They had it set up so the Hodgson freight truck would meet the Greyhound when it got to Williams Lake and Bev would catch a ride to Tatlayoko with the mail truck driver. But the bus was late, and when Bev arrived in Williams Lake she learned the Hodgson truck had left two hours earlier.

"I started to cry," she said. "Then the most wonderful woman, Rita Rife, took me home. They knew the Hayneses and knew that Billy Berwin was going to school in Williams Lake."

Bev waited with the Rifes until Billy got out of school and he arranged for a ride out to Tatlayoko. That's how Bev came to the Chilcotin and never left, and how a short time later she met Tommy Lulua for the first time.

Bev Butler lived with Del Naomi and Harry Haynes for two years until she met Lee Butler. They fell in love and got married in 1957, just as Bev turned seventeen.

"I was working at Tatla Lake for Joy Graham, and Lee's sister Elora was working for Margaret Graham in the Big House," Bev said. "Elora brought me down to the Butler Ranch for the weekend, and that's where I met Lee for the first time. We couldn't keep our eyes off each other."

Bev said Del Naomi Haynes was special to her.

"She told me I was the daughter she never had. Auntie Del cooked different than Momma Dack. Mom Dack was very English and she boiled everything. Auntie Del knew how to cook food and it was really good."

Del Naomi Haynes, Alex Paxton and Jim Holt on beef drive. Photo courtesy Harry Haynes

Bev and Lee Butler at their home in the West Branch Valley. Sage Birchwater photo

Lucy Dagg Dester Sulin

Some said she was 120 years old. Others claimed she was 107. She once told me she was a little younger than Chiwid, who, according to church records, was born in 1903. So go figure. At any rate, when Lucy Dagg Dester Sulin died on April 24, 2001, she was close to 100 years old. And she had a good death by all measures: family members gathered around, drumming and singing for her in her Tŝilhqot'in language at Deni House in Williams Lake.

Birth records in the old days were informal. Lucy was already old enough to carry a backpack into the mountains when her parents bothered to get her baptized by the Oblate priest Father Francois Marie Thomas at Redstone Flats. Her stepdad, George Turner, wasn't particularly religious. He was known to keep a low profile, so attending "priest time" to get his stepdaughter registered was not a huge priority. And Lucy was classified as "non-status" despite her mother, Louisa One-Eye, being Tŝilhqot'in. Her biological dad, George Dagg, was Scottish, and her stepdad was American. Paternity carried weight in those days in determining Indigenous status. On her mother's side, Louisa One-Eye was the daughter of Tŝilhqot'in Chief One-Eye of Kleena Kleene. One Eye Lake is named after him. Louisa's mother was Dakelh from the country north of Anahim Lake, so the language spoken in the One-Eye household was a mix of Tŝilhqot'in and Dakelh.

George Dagg spent several years in the Chilcotin and fathered a number of children with different Tŝilhqot'in mothers. Billy Dagg, half-brother to Eagle Lake Henry, an influential Tŝilhqot'in man around Naghatalhchuẑ (Big Eagle/Choelquoit Lake), was one. Celestine Guichon Dagg Squinas was another. She married Thomas Squinas and together they had ten kids. Then there was Cas "Coyote" Dagg, half-brother to Chiwid, Scotty Gregg, Madeline Elkins and Ollie Nukalow, who died young as a teenager from tuberculosis.

Thomas Squinas, who was born in 1906, said Lucy and Chiwid were close in age. Lucy once told me her first memory of Chiwid was down at Clearwater Lake when they were both young girls.

"We were trapping fish where the creek flows out of the lake," she said. "I remember Chiwid's uncle Little Johnny looking for her. He had a big stick because Chiwid had run off with some boys. Little Johnny raised Chiwid because her mother, Loozap, was deaf and couldn't speak."

When I met Lucy she was married to Willie Sulin at Towdystan. This was her second marriage. She and Willie had three children, Edith Duteau and Eddie and Tony Sulin, and they had also adopted their grandson Larry Sulin, Edith's oldest child. Larry's biological dad was freight truck driver Don "Squeak" Widdis, who travelled through the

Lucy Dagg Dester Sulin laughs after "blowing" out her candles on her birthday cake by waving a paper plate. Sage Birchwater photo

Chilcotin from Williams Lake to Bella Coola. Larry's existence wasn't widely known in Williams Lake, where Widdis lived with his family, but in Towdystan his nickname was Squeak.

Lucy's first husband, Baptiste Dester, was a Tŝilhqot'in man from Nemiah Valley. He made his way to Kleena Kleene when he was sixteen years old, and eventually he and Lucy got married. Baptiste trapped down the Klinaklini River with Lucy's stepfather, George Turner, all the way to Knight Inlet on the coast and up the north fork of the Klinaklini into Knot Lakes country.

Lucy's grandfather Chief One-Eye also trapped down the Klinaklini before Lucy was born. Lucy's granddaughter Joanne Gregg said old One-Eye, her great-great-grandfather, made it to the mouth of the Klinaklini.

"He taught a Tŝilhqot'in song to the Kwakwaka'wakw people there," she told me. "Old One-Eye's brother was Chief Anaham of Stuic [Stuie] in the Bella Coola Valley. Then Anaham moved up to Nagwentl'un [Tŝilhqot'in for Anahim Lake] and later on to Alexis Creek, where the Tl'etinqox community is today."

Those are the family ties that bind the people in the region.

Baptiste and George would be gone months at a time, covering hundreds of kilometres on snowshoes through that precipitous terrain. At Christmas they would pull their marten traps and be home for a few weeks before heading out to trap beaver and muskrats until spring.

STATUS AND THE INDIAN ACT

The Indian Act, established by the government of Canada in 1876, was designed to eliminate Indigenous cultures in favour of assimilation into Euro-Canadian society. While having status under the act does convey certain benefits for Indigenous people, such as access to reserve land and territory and various funding opportunities for education, housing and health care, many discriminatory practices were governed by the act. A Status Indian under the Indian Act could not own Crown land and could not consume alcohol, and Indigenous women lost their status if they married a non-status man. Perhaps most sinister of all, the children of Status Indians were required to attend industrial residential schools run by various religious organizations.

Baptiste Dester in front of his cabin at Clearwater Lake near Kleena Kleene. Photo courtesy the Dester family

Like Lucy, Baptiste didn't have his Indigenous status. His mother, Yeleucy, was Tŝilhqot'in, but his biological father was an Englishman, Riske Creek storekeeper and postmaster Gerald Dester. It's likely Gerald never knew he had a son. As the story goes, he was off in England when Baptiste was born in 1901, and he died shortly after returning to Canada in 1902. Yet Father Francois Marie Thomas sniffed out Baptiste's non-Indigenous paternity and baptized him accordingly with the Dester moniker. On that basis he may have been denied his Indigenous status.

BAPTISTE'S PATERNITY

Some in-depth sleuthing into the past, by a Lower Mainland man tracing the roots of his wife's family history, resulted in changing history for literally hundreds of people living in the Cariboo Chilcotin.

Over the internet, John Macdonald of Delta tracked down Petrina Dester of Bella Coola. He was searching for descendants of Gerald Dester, the long-lost great-grandfather of his wife, Brenda.

According to Macdonald's family records, Gerald came to Canada from England in 1883 to work on the Canadian Pacific Railway, then settled at Riske Creek in the Chilcotin, where he was a store owner and postmaster for several years. He fathered four children there before returning to England in 1900 with his oldest daughter, Isabel (born in 1889), his second wife, Caroline, and their infant daughter, Evelyn (born in 1898).

A year later he returned to Canada alone, leaving his wife and children in England, and he died at Alkali Lake a year after that, on November 8, 1902.

But when John Macdonald spoke to Petrina Dester, there was a disconnect between Gerald Dester and the man Petrina was related to through marriage. Baptiste Dester of Kleena Kleene, the grandfather of Petrina's husband, Elliott, was the son of a man they all knew as George Dester. That was the accepted family lore and official historical record in the Chilcotin.

Through his meticulous research, Macdonald was able to discover that Gerald Dester and George Dester were indeed the same man. This opened the floodgates for a resounding family reunion at the Denisiqi centre in Williams Lake on October 13, 2007. Four representatives of the thirty living descendants of Evelyn Dester—John and Brenda Macdonald, Valery Chambers and Geoff Chambers—met up with about 200 of the 520 living descendants of Baptiste Dester and his half-sister, Lottie Johnny.

"I came from a family of two," Valery told the gathering. "I didn't have a dad. I just love to find all you people I'm related to."

To appreciate the significance of the Gerald (George) Dester family reunion, you have to understand the clash and melding of cultures that occurred on the British Columbia and Cariboo Chilcotin frontier during the latter half of the nineteenth century.

When Gerald Dester arrived in Riske Creek, he took Jessie Peltwashaata as his Tŝilhqot'in wife. Together they had Isabel, born in 1889, and Lottie, born in 1894.

Then in 1897 he married Caroline Magee, the daughter of British immigrants who had settled in New Westminster in 1861. But Caroline did not stay long at Riske Creek and moved to Vancouver before giving birth to their daughter, Evelyn, on January 31, 1898.

In November 1900, Gerald took his eleven-year-old daughter, Isabel, back to England to give her a British education, but before he left he conceived a child with Yeleucy, a Tŝilhqot'in woman from Nemiah Valley. According to baptismal records, Baptiste Dester was born in August 1901, while Gerald was in England.

The jury is out as to whether Gerald Dester even knew about his son, Baptiste. But what we know for sure is that the mothers and extended Tŝilhqot'in families of Lottie and Baptiste nurtured Gerald's offspring to become respected citizens of their community. Five hundred living relatives are evidence of that.

(I authored this article on the Dester family reunion in the Williams Lake Tribune, *October 18, 2007.)*

At least that's one story explaining why Baptiste wasn't granted his status. In another, he willingly gave up his enfranchisement as an Indigenous person so he could own Crown land, and Lucy lost her status when she married him. Baptiste was a forward-thinking man who wanted every advantage for himself. From the money he made from his lucrative trapping ventures he lived well throughout the year. He was one of the first citizens of the West Chilcotin to own a motor car. Not many people had vehicles in those days.

Lucy and Baptiste had seven children together: Annie Elkins, Josephine Gregg, Rosie Boyd Morpaw, Theresa Dester, David Dester, Mack Dester and Billy Dester. During the summers they would camp around the plateau, hunting and fishing and taking the odd ranch job cowboying, putting up hay or building fence. Baptiste and Lucy shared the workload.

Josephine Gregg, Lucy and Baptiste's second child, shed some insight into their busy lifestyle. She said her own birth occurred while her family was on a goat-hunting expedition in the Klinaklini mountains in the fall of 1925. Lucy was assisted in the birth by her mother, Louisa, and her half-sister Mary Ann Turner Ross. Like many Indigenous families in those days, Josephine was born on the trail as her family was engaged in their daily activity for survival. The joke is that when Father Thomas came to register her at "priest time" nine or ten months later, he got the month of her birth wrong. Through some miscommunication or disregard, he incorrectly concluded she was born on October 20, 1925, and that's what he entered onto her official birth record. Josephine always laughed, insisting this couldn't be true. "I was probably born in September because my parents wouldn't have been hunting goats up in the mountains in October. There was too much snow at that time of year," she told me.

To add insult to injury, Father Thomas incorrectly wrote her name as

"Saraphine" on her birth documents, causing confusion many years later when Josephine's family attempted to obtain her Indigenous status.

When Annie and Josephine were old enough to go to school, the family moved to Tatla Lake for a couple of years.

"We went to school there for two years, in 1931 and 1932. I was doing pretty good but my mother didn't like it there," Josephine told me. "So my mom and dad bought a little ranch at Anahim Lake to raise cattle. My uncle, Lucy's half-brother Billy Dagg, was ranch foreman for Andy Christensen at Cless Pocket Ranch."

Josephine Gregg with author Sage Birchwater at the book launch of Gumption & Grit [Caitlin Press, 2009] in Williams Lake. Sage Birchwater collection

In 1939 Lucy and Baptiste split up and sold their Anahim Lake ranch and divided the money. Baptiste moved back to Kleena Kleene with twenty-five head of cattle, and Lucy got together with Willie Sulin at Towdystan. Josephine said that after her parents separated, she and her siblings scattered throughout the country.

"My youngest brother, Billy Dester, was only two years old and he stayed with Lucy and Willie. David was six and moved in with our dad at Kleena Kleene, where he had pre-empted a ranch at Clearwater Lake. It was really difficult for David to keep up, running after Dad on his trapline. When he was older he moved away from the Chilcotin for good."

BIRTH OF A CAREER

I was living in a cabin tent with my family at Thelma Petrie's place at Clearwater Lake near Kleena Kleene in the fall and winter of 1983–84 when Lucy Sulin showed up one day on horseback. At seventy-eight years old she had ridden the whole way from Towdystan, a distance of thirty or forty kilometres, to buy a sack of flour and some groceries at Thelma's store. There was snow on the ground. I was quite impressed by her endurance, stamina and independence. This incident kind of launched my journalism career. There was a story here but I didn't own a camera to take a photo, so I asked *Williams Lake Tribune* editor Diana French if there was an old camera kicking around the newspaper office I could borrow. She gave me an old relic she had with a broken light meter.

"Just frame your shots above and below what you think the lighting might be," she suggested.

So that's how it began. Thanks to Lucy Sulin and Diana French, my work documenting times and happenings in the West Chilcotin was off and running.

LUCY'S BIRTHDAY BASH

Lucy was ageless, it seemed. On October 8, 1990, her family decided it was time for her to have a birthday party. It was to be a surprise affair. Apparently in her eighty-six years she'd never had a birthday celebration before, so they tagged it as a family reunion and rented Anahim Lake Community Hall.

There was a potlatch-style feast with people coming from all directions: Bella Coola, Kamloops, Williams Lake, Fort St. James and places all across the Chilcotin. They cooked eleven turkeys, two hams and seventy kilograms of potatoes and baked a big cake. All seven of Lucy's surviving children were there, along with most of her fifty-three grandchildren, seventy-five great-grandchildren and eight great-great-grandchildren. Five generations and over one hundred people all together in one place.

Stories were told of Lucy's unusual life, how she was born in a traditional brush house near Towdystan around 1904, and how she spent a vigorous life trapping, hunting and gathering what she needed from the land. She had an intimate knowledge of both edible and medicinal plants, and where and what time of year they could be harvested. Whenever someone in her family got sick, Lucy would send someone to the mountains to bring back certain plants. She knew her plants well and made medicine out of pitch mixed with bear grease or eulachon grease. Too stinky sometimes, this ointment was used for burns and chest colds. There was one very powerful plant for diseases that she used called *helhdilh* (false hellebore, *Veratrum viride*). It had many uses, but you had to be careful because it was poisonous. You had to chew the root but spit out the juice and not use too much.

Lucy also knew about traditional foods from the land. She taught her kids that when they got really hungry there is a mountain pine cone with edible seeds (whitebark pine, *Pinus albicaulis*). Or you could chew "Indian bubble gum"—the pitch from spruce or lodgepole pine trees—or scrape the inner bark from pine trees in springtime. It doesn't taste good but it helps if you are hungry. Before potatoes people would eat a certain kind of root, and there was a plant you could make something like flour out of. Teas were made from certain roots and leaves, and soap could be made from white alkaline dirt.

In Lucy's time people had to travel great distances to get all the things they needed for survival. Often Lucy and her husband would be gone two weeks at a time trapping or picking up supplies like sugar, rice or flour while their children stayed home by themselves, often quite hungry. Back then this was normal.

Lucy worked hard all her life haying and raising cattle, horses, sheep, chickens and even goats. She loved her animals and used to talk to them all the time. One time she kept a pet steer that grew to be as big as a bull. People often teased her about it. They said they were going to steal it because they were hungry. Finally Lucy butchered the animal and gave all the meat away to her family but wouldn't eat any herself.

"I don't want to eat my own pet," she protested.

One day Lucy had a tooth that was bothering her, so she dug it out herself using her pocket knife. Her granddaughter Joanne Gregg was there and told me what happened:

"It was at my mom's place in Tatla Lake, and Grandma only had a couple of wonky old teeth left. She got one out with her pocket knife. I knew there was a dentist at Anahim Lake and I called him up. He stopped by my mom's place and pulled Grandma's last remaining teeth. He didn't bother using freezing because they were so loose he just popped them out. He didn't want her risking infection by going after them with her pocket knife. Grandma Lucy always laughed about how she got the dentist to give her a house call."

Like her mother, Louisa One-Eye Turner, Lucy was fiercely independent and self-reliant. When her family needed meat, she didn't hesitate to go out and hunt a moose. She would take two horses, go out and hunt by herself and bring back a moose. Then her daughters would help her cut it up for drying. Life on the high Chilcotin Plateau demanded ingenuity and determination. Everything you had came from hard work.

Lucy recalled the years she and Baptiste Dester had their Model T Ford. One year they took a trip to Prince George.

"Sometimes the road was good," she told me, "but mostly it was rough and it took a long time to get there. In those days you didn't need car insurance or a driver's licence, and the Chilcotin Road was so narrow that branches hit the windows on both sides. So you couldn't stick your head out the window."

Baptiste did most of the driving on the longer trips to Williams Lake or beyond, but Lucy sometimes drove the car around Kleena Kleene or Tatla Lake. Mostly, though, she preferred riding her horse.

One time when Lucy was close to seventy years old, she bought a horse from her half-brother Timothy Baptiste at Redstone Flats and rode the animal all the way back to Towdystan. It took her two days. She had to get back right away because she had hungry grandkids staying at her house. The first day she made it to her son Mack Dester's place at Kleena Kleene. Then she continued home the next day, another five hours in the saddle. She said in the old days it was nothing to go on horseback from Towdystan to Redbrush for the Easter dance. It was quicker taking the old Chilanko River trail because it was sixty kilometres shorter than the highway through Tatla Lake.

At Lucy's birthday gathering, some people were surprised to learn how many siblings Lucy had. Besides Celestine Guichon Dagg Squinas, Billy Dagg and Cas "Coyote" Dagg on her father's side, there was Timothy Baptiste, George Turner Jr. and Mary Anne Turner Ross on her mother's side. Also, Louisa One-Eye had given birth to four other kids as a younger woman: Yancy One-Eye, Johnny One-Eye, Eddie Stillas and Mark Stillas. Josephine Gregg said Eddie and Mark had been adopted by Ulkatcho families before Lucy was born. Later in life, Lucy took care of one of her older brothers in his old age before he passed away.

Once people had eaten their fill of the main course, a gigantic cake was brought out with over eighty candles burning. Youngsters waited spellbound to see whether their great matriarch would keel over from exhaustion trying to blow out all the candles in one breath. But Lucy fooled them. With a mischievous twinkle in her eye, she picked up a paper plate and with a couple of quick flicks of her wrist she extinguished all eighty-plus candles without exerting so much as a small puff of air. Everyone had a good laugh.

One time when Lucy was chasing her chickens around her yard, a family member asked her why she was working so hard.

"It keeps you young," she laughed.

Many times she spoke of a plant she would eat that "keeps you strong." As her years advanced, she quipped: "I must have eaten too much of that plant."

WILLIE SULIN LISTENS TO HIS HORSE

In the spring of 1984 an emergency ensued in the Ulkatcho community when eighteen-year-old Tory Jack was reported missing. It was late May and he was staying with his grandmother Susan Cahoose at Fish Trap, where the Dean River empties out of Nimpo Lake, when he decided to walk through the bush to meet up with his dad, Gene Jack, in Anahim Lake. The distance following the Dean River is about sixteen kilometres.

It's not that Tory was a novice at travelling in the bush. He and his dad lived in one of the more remote and wilder corners of Ulkatcho territory, one hundred kilometres north of Anahim Lake in the Entiako headwaters north of Ulkatcho Village. They had a few head of horses and cut hay for them there, and they also ran a trapline. Gene was one of the last prolific trappers in the Ulkatcho community, and Tory was very bush wise.

So when Tory took off through the bush to go and see his dad, nobody was too concerned. But when he hadn't shown up after two days, his family realized he was lost. On June 1 the Ulkatcho community initiated a search.

Willie Sulin with his horse Gypsy, who helped him track down Tory Jack, who had been lost in the woods for over a week near Nimpo Lake. Sage Birchwater photo

They hired a helicopter, and numerous people went out on horseback to comb the area where Tory's footprints had last been seen. A base camp to support the searchers was set up by Tory's grandmother Susan Cahoose along the Morrison Meadow Road. Susan reasoned that her grandson might be attracted by the camp activity, campfire smoke or smell of food cooking and find his way out of the bush.

On June 3 Anahim Lake search and rescue volunteers coordinated a larger search and the RCMP hired a second helicopter. The next day, ground searchers came across what they thought were the fresh tracks of the missing man.

Joanne Gregg was one of the searchers.

"We were way up past Morrison Meadow, past Dick Wright's and Andy Lendvoy's places," she told me,

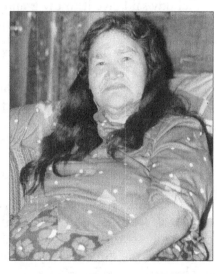

Susan Sulin Cahoose, grandmother of Tory Jack, set up a support camp for the searchers looking for her grandson. Sage Birchwater photo

Willie Sulin with his grandson Willie Andy. Sage Birchwater photo

"and we saw Tory's fresh footprints in the mud. We made a map and somebody said give it to my grandpa Willie Sulin. Willie was a registered game guide and he knew that country like the back of his hand. The next day Willie and Herb Parker rode up by saddle horse from Towdystan, and by noon the next day they found Tory alive and well."

Willie recounted to me what happened:

"We moved into the thick bush where the tracks were last seen, about five hours by saddle horse from the nearest road where the base camp was located. Tory had walked a long ways. He must have crossed the trail to go down for a drink of water or something, because my horse smelled his scent."

Willie said it was the actions of his horse that led him to the missing man.

"My horse kept looking off to one side, so I kept heading him in that direction. We followed Tory's scent for a quarter mile through the thick bush until my horse finally stopped. At first I didn't see anything and then I looked in the direction my horse was looking and spotted Tory standing beneath a tree."

At first the missing man was frightened and ran off as Willie and Herb started approaching. This is a common reaction of people who get lost. They get bushed and fearful of other people.

"He was like a wild man when he first saw me," Willie continued. "I called his name and suddenly he recognized me. 'Oh, you,' he said, and he stopped running. I asked him why he was hiding and running away, and he said, 'I thought you'd be mad at me.' I offered him a sandwich but he wasn't hungry, even though he had been missing eight days and nights by that time without a coat or food. All he wanted was a drink of coffee."

Willie fired three shots with his rifle and made a signal fire, which was quickly spotted by the helicopter, and Tory was whisked away to the nursing clinic in Anahim Lake. Apparently there was little wrong with him other than being cold and hungry. Willie said Tory stayed alive by walking around at night and sleeping during the day when temperatures were warmer. He also ate roots that his dad had taught him about to survive in the bush.

"The thick treads on his boots were worn pretty smooth, and it froze at night," Willie added. "It also rained and snowed. It's a wonder he wasn't attacked by a grizzly."

Corporal Neil Taylor of the RCMP said he was impressed with how well the Ulkatcho people conducted the search by setting up the camp to supply food and support to the ground searchers. Search and rescue coordinator Randy Baxter was also praised for his efforts in mobilizing the search party.

But the greatest accolades belonged to Gypsy, the horse who smelled the missing man, and the bush-wise wisdom of game guide Willie Sulin, who was smart enough to listen to his horse.

REMEMBERING BAPTISTE DESTER

Baptiste Dester was pushing ninety years old when he passed away at Deni House in Williams Lake in March 1990. Many people gathered in his memory, and he was praised for his strength of character and goodwill. He was a man of his word, always willing to help others.

Baptiste was an exceptional woodsman, trapper and hunter. Besides trapping and hunting for himself, he guided hunters in the fall for Jim Mackill, owner of the Kleena Kleene Lodge on One Eye Lake, and for Bob Stewart of Stewart's Resort on Nimpo Lake.

Rancher Fred Brink, in an article I wrote in the *Williams Lake Tribune* on May 10, 1990, praised Baptiste for being completely honest.

"He was a first-class log builder. He was real independent and worked mostly for himself when I first knew him."

Bernie Gano, in the same article, also had kind words for Baptiste.

"We only had one horse for our two children when we first came to the country in 1958. Baptiste noticed them riding double and said he had an extra horse he could spare. A short time later he arrived at our place leading this horse behind him. He wouldn't take any money for it."

Bernie built his place on raw land he bought behind Caribou Flats along the McClinchy River. He said Baptiste was very helpful and especially generous with his knowledge of the country.

"He always gave you a straight answer when you wanted to know something."

Bernie was able to repay Baptiste for his generosity many years later, after Baptiste suffered a debilitating stroke that cost him his ability to speak and the use of one arm.

"He'd come to our place and I'd shoe his horse for him," he said.

Baptiste's grandson Garry Gregg told me his grandfather worked so much he was hardly ever home.

"Grandpa used to go into his trapline in the fall and didn't come out until June sometimes. Mom said she never seen him for almost a year one time. Grandpa used to have his guiding camp fairly close to where Bernie Gano built his place. He used to make hay there every year. Then he got Bernie to guide for him one fall. The next summer when Grandpa went to make hay, Bernie had claimed it."

Joanne Gregg said that back in the old days Tŝilhqot'in people didn't claim the land; they just used it.

"Every family had their territory. We just used the land in that territory; we didn't claim it. When Baptiste got enfranchised so he could

Baptiste Dester and Clarence Mackill with a trophy grizzly. Photo courtesy the Dester family

buy land, he still stayed with the old way. He used the land over such a vast area it didn't make sense for him to claim every little piece of it," she told me.

Kate McDonough and her husband, Mike, met Baptiste in 1969 when they began living at the Poet Place, a small ranch ten kilometres down the Klinaklini Valley. She told me Baptiste was a significant part of their lives there.

"He'd already had his stroke by the time we met him and it was hard to understand him at first, but we learned how to talk with him. He moved down to the Poet Place and lived in one of the cabins for a while. He was very generous to us and gave us a wonderful horse, Mr. Natural. He also gave us a moose he had shot."

Ed Ober was a partner with Bob Stewart in the early 1950s when he and Bob started what eventually became known as Stewart's Lodge and Camps on Nimpo Lake. In those days they called it Nimpo Lake Camp. Baptiste Dester lived just down the road at Clearwater Lake and provided guide outfitting services to the fledgling lodge owners. He also taught them how to hunt and where to go for game. Ed said the last time he saw Baptiste was in late 1956.

"I gave him a ride to visit a rancher in Walla Walla, Washington, who had hunted with us that fall. He was impressed with how Baptiste got along with his horses. Also everyone really liked Baptiste, who was a man of a few well-chosen words," Ed told me.

"On a mountain goat hunt with a couple of hunters, one pack horse got belly down in a soft patch, a bog or whatever," he recalled. "We removed the pack boxes, and after much huffing and puffing the horse quit trying to get out. Baptiste grabbed a length of rope and started whacking the horse's hind end hard. The horse started trying again. *Whack, whack!* Harder yet. Soft-hearted me: 'I don't think the horse likes that, Baptiste ...'

"'He don't like it,' Baptiste said.

"With another lunge the horse got out of the muck. Baptiste put the pack boxes on and without a word we kept going."

BEAR BAIT, AS TOLD BY ED OBER

"Nimpo Lake Camp was busy. It was late July and we were fully booked. Every cabin was rented, every boat was rented, and the fishing was very good. It was the type of situation you hear about but seldom find. The income from fishing paid the taxes, but the real money was from hunting. The number one attraction was hunting grizzly bear. In the average year only 3 percent of licensed grizzly hunters even see a bear. Hunting grizzly bear is an ego trip for the newly rich.

"Avalanches kill some deer, moose, mountain goats and caribou each winter. This is called 'winterkill' by the Game Department. When grizzly bears come out of hibernation each spring, they head for areas with winterkill. Most of the winterkill is in areas where hunting is difficult, so in an attempt to attract bears it was the practice to lead an old lame horse into the bush where a bear is most likely to be found and shoot it. It took several weeks to age properly, so we figured we needed to get a head start on the season.

"I saddled up one of Baptiste's horses and rode the ten miles to the Capoose spread. I didn't see anyone so I tied up my horse and walked over to a split-rail fence and was leaning on the top rail.

"'Good horse, most thirty-two,' said a voice behind me. I continued leaning on the rail, neither turning nor answering. I knew the voice. The sun was hot and it was not a hurrying kind of day. Ogie Capoose no doubt knew I had ridden over to look at horses. Otherwise I would have driven. He even may have suspected the kind of horse I was looking for.

"Finally I answered: 'That bay over by the stack of fence posts, thirty-two you say? Looks mostly dead. I can take him with me to save you the digging. Won't charge.'

Then I turned, looking at Ogie, the horse wrangler.

"'Good horse, just old,' he answered.

"'Ogie, I'm looking for an old horse to use as bear bait. He only needs to be able to walk up into the Rainbow Mountains. Something for about five dollars.'

"'Twenty dollars,' he replied.

"'Twenty bucks for that broken-down nag? I can buy a horse to compete in the Calgary Stampede for twenty dollars,' I countered.

"'Listen close,' he replied. 'You want an old horse cheap. This one is thirty-two years old, maybe more. Twenty dollars is cheap. He's a little sway-backed and skin and bones poor. You notice, but the grizzly won't notice. His name is Smoke. Smoke is my favourite pack horse. He's all I have for sale.'

"'You old thief, I need a horse. Let's split it. How about ten dollars?' I tried. Ogie didn't answer. He just stood there smiling and waiting. I waited and smiled back, then slowly handed him the twenty dollars, hoping for a change of heart. I put a halter on Smoke and started back to Nimpo Lake. Smoke led easily. He was no problem and seemed to enjoy the trip.

"Then we learned the Game Department had closed the grizzly bear hunt that spring. The previous winter there had been an abnormally low amount of snow. Because of this there had been few avalanches, resulting in fewer winterkills and a reduced food supply for cubs and yearling bears. These were the most vulnerable, but the entire season was closed.

"Smoke was turned out with the other horses at Baptiste's place a few miles down toward Kleena Kleene. He was content hanging around the yard and helping himself to the cattle's hay. Most horses not in constant use drift off into the bush. When they are needed they are rounded up, often against their will. Sometimes they are hard to find. It wasn't a very good system, but it eliminated the feed cost.

"Fall moose-hunting season arrived with the usual problems. The most pressing problem was rounding up enough pack horses. Our first group of hunters was ready to go, and we still needed a pack horse. Smoke was hanging around taking it all in. Baptiste, who was the head guide, said Smoke looked bad but was well fed and lively. 'I wonder if he can pack much weight?'

"'We can pack him light on this trip and see how he does,' I answered. 'We won't need him for bear bait this year.'

"So we gave him a slightly lighter pack than the others. On the trail Smoke just walked along enjoying the company. All of the situations like yellow jackets, bear scat, bear smell, soft swamp, loose shale, were calmly dealt with. The other half-broke pack horses would go crazy with any of these, often throwing off their pack boxes.

"The second day on the trail, pack loads are switched around to try to match the temperaments of the pack horses. The real knot-heads you loaded with as much weight as they could handle. This was unbreakable items. You wanted this type to be tired out.

"Smoke had trotted to the elite status. The term used in the trade is 'egg horse.' You want fragile items on the steadiest pack horse you have. Every hunt usually had a dozen cartons of fresh eggs. You wanted them to arrive at the base camp whole. In addition to eggs, the egg horse would pack other fragile items such as cameras, field glasses and assorted liquor.

"One day I told Baptiste I could see why he was called Smoke. 'He can pick his way over windfall and through thick pine trees like poetry in motion. Never rubbing a pack box off against a tree. Just like smoke. I have never seen any horse this calm unless he was dead.'

"Then I started bragging about my talent for judging pack horses, but Baptiste had quit listening and was walking away.

"Smoke was used on every hunt that fall. At the end of the hunting season, all horses except personal saddle horses were turned out again. They were expected to fend for themselves until spring, grazing wild meadows, willow groves and whatever they could find to hold them through the winter. Some made it through the winter and some didn't. Each year the same cycle. Half-broken horses rounded up and put to use.

"Smoke's method of fending for himself was different. He would visit cattle ranches in the area. The ranchers would see him that winter in with the cattle. He moved from one ranch to the next, careful to never overstay his welcome. In cattle country most ranchers didn't worry about a little hay.

"One spring as the snow was melting and the short winter days with the bitter cold were only memories, Baptiste mentioned he hadn't seen Smoke lately. 'Maybe he is afraid they will have a grizzly bear hunt this year.'

"I said he was probably stuck in some rancher's hay fence and told him I'd ask around, and if no one has him I'd grab one of his horses and ride around a little until I find him.

"'You don't find bear bait that can pack eggs every day,' I said as I headed out.

"In the low brush-covered hills to the west, before the mountains start, I found his remains, covered with a pile of leaves. Grizzly sign told me his sad ending. Smoke had been purchased as bear bait, but he earned extra years as the best egg horse in the Chilcotin, even as he met his end as bear bait.

"I rode back to camp with a heavy heart, wishing he could have died asleep, bedded down in some rancher's haystack."

THE EDWARDS FAMILY OF LONESOME LAKE

Ralph Edwards was a household name when I first arrived in the Cariboo Chilcotin Coast in 1973. The 1957 book *Crusoe of Lonesome Lake*, by Leland Stowe, impacted his family's reclusive life, putting Ralph, his wife, Ethel, and their three kids, Stanley, John and Trudy, into the public spotlight. After that they received a continual flow of fan mail from people curious about how they were living.

By the time I got there, Ralph had been carving out a unique existence in the Coast Mountain wilds of the upper Atnarko Valley for over sixty years. One of the family's more noteworthy contributions was saving the trumpeter swans that wintered there. North America's largest waterfowl species was on the brink of extinction from overhunting when Ralph established his pre-emption at Lonesome Lake in January 1913. Eventually he and his family started feeding them in winter. That meant packing thousands of pounds of barley over the rugged trail and across the lake into their remote homestead. Unlike the passenger pigeon that went extinct by 1914, the trumpeter swan population rebounded thanks in large part to the Edwards family's dedication.

The faint hope of a railway coming to the Central Coast port of Bella Coola inspired Ralph Edwards to establish his farm at Lonesome Lake. He figured that with rail transport to bring his produce to market, it might actually make farming in that remote location profitable. But any chance of a railway coming their way was quashed when the Grand Trunk Pacific Railway between Jasper and Prince Rupert was chosen as the preferred route for Canada's second transcontinental rail crossing to the Pacific Ocean. Its last spike was pounded in 1914, and the list of other proposed routes was taken off the books.

Ralph Edwards was born in Hot Springs, North Carolina, in 1891 and was raised in North Carolina and Massachusetts by various members of his family. His Seventh-day Adventist parents were medical missionaries, and Ralph spent three years in India with them before his family moved back to the United States. While his parents moved around the country getting the medical training needed for their calling, Ralph was shunted from one family to another. This included living with his grandparents, aunts and uncles. In the process he learned to be self-reliant, hard-working and self-educating, and these attributes served him well in the wilderness of British Columbia.

Ralph was twenty-one years old when he took the coastal steamship from Vancouver to Bella Coola in August 1912. He was looking for free land to settle. But when he stepped off the boat, he learned that most of the good farmland in the Bella Coola Valley had already been taken by Norwegian and Seventh-day Adventist settlers.

Undaunted, he acquired a couple of horses, loaded them with everything he owned and started up the valley. Most newcomers seeking land were passing through the Bella Coola Valley and moving north, following the ancient grease trail route to Ootsa Lake.

Vehicles could make it only twenty-eight miles (forty-five kilometres) up the valley to Firvale, where a community of Seventh-day Adventists had settled. Beyond that, access was on horseback or by foot. The Nuxalk-Dakelh Grease Trail followed by Alexander Mackenzie in 1793 climbed the steep switchbacks of Burnt Bridge Creek just beyond Firvale and crossed the Rainbow Mountains. The main trail farther up the valley followed the Bella Coola River to Stuie, where two major tributaries, the glacier-fed Talchako from the south and the Atnarko from the east, joined to form the Bella Coola River. The major trail out of the valley beyond there continued up the Atnarko for twelve miles (twenty kilometres) to Hotnarko River, where it climbed the steep Precipice Trail to the Chilcotin Plateau. Ralph decided to seek his fortunes up the Atnarko Valley.

In Firvale Ralph met the Ratcliff clan, two pairs of brothers, Milo and John and their cousins Frank and Walter. All were Americans and recent arrivals from Oregon. It was Frank Ratcliff who took Ralph to Lonesome Lake in October.

They proceeded by foot up the steep switchback trail to Turner Lake, where Hunlen Falls spills out of the lake and drops 1,300 feet (400 metres) into the Atnarko Valley. They rafted up Turner Lake, where Frank brought Ralph to a viewpoint overlooking the 7-mile (11-kilometre), S-shaped Lonesome Lake 1,000 feet (300 metres) below. At that time the lake had no official name on Canadian maps. It is Ralph who was given credit for naming it.

The men bushwhacked down the mountainside to where the Atnarko River flows into Lonesome Lake, and that's where Ralph staked his 160-acre (65-hectare) pre-emption he later called the Birches. Two months later he got word his application was approved.

On January 10, 1913, Ralph and Frank headed out to Lonesome Lake to build his cabin. This time the two men continued up the Atnarko to

Lonesome Lake, which had frozen over, and they dragged Ralph's 600 pounds (270 kilograms) of supplies down the ice using a homemade sleigh. It took them three days to do the log work for his 10-by-14-foot (3-by-4.25-metre) cabin and a bit longer to cut cedar shakes and construct the roof. Soon Ralph was able to move in and start carving out his legacy. Slowly and methodically, he felled big trees and pulled the stumps with winches and come-alongs. By spring he had cleared 2 acres (0.8 hectares) of land.

During the summer of 1913 Ralph got a job working on a crew stringing the new telegraph line across the Chilcotin Plateau from 150 Mile House to Bella Coola. He earned three dollars a day plus room and board.

Ralph Edwards, circa 1940. Photo published on page 146 in Trudy Turner's memoir, *Packtrains & Airplanes: Memories of Lonesome Lake* [Hancock House, 2012]

"The job entailed stringing a single line of cold drawn galvanized number eight wire from tree to tree," Ralph described in his 1979 memoir, *Ralph Edwards of Lonesome Lake*, as told to Ed Gould.[2] "Where there were no trees, poles were dug into the ground. Linemen topped and trimmed the trees and sideblocks were nailed onto the trees or poles and insulators were screwed onto the sideblocks. Big coils of wire were put on turntables and the ends pulled over the rough ground from tree to tree."

At the end of the summer Ralph returned to Lonesome Lake to continue working on his homestead. He dug and fenced a large garden and began experimenting with fruit trees that could survive in the microclimate of the upper Atnarko Valley.

"Over the years I planted and experimented with over forty varieties of fruit trees before I found an adequate number to survive the winter," he stated.[3]

When Canada entered the First World War in 1914, Ralph stayed focused on hacking his homestead out of the wilderness. When Walter Ratcliff decided to join the Canadian Army, he gave Ralph his dog Whitie to look after. Ralph appreciated the canine company, but what he really

---

2   Ralph A. Edwards and Ed Gould, *Ralph Edwards of Lonesome Lake* (Surrey, BC: Hancock House, 1979), 50.

3   Edwards and Gould, *Ralph Edwards*, 62.

wanted was female companionship to share in his wilderness paradise. He had exchanged many letters with his childhood sweetheart, Helen Cathie from North Carolina, and he hoped one day to bring her to the home he was building.

After spending another long winter alone at Lonesome Lake, Ralph decided it was time to act on his feelings. He wrote Helen and told her he was coming to see her. Her letters had been passionate and encouraging, and he wanted to tell her in person about his adventures. But when Ralph arrived, Helen told him she wasn't cut out to be a wilderness bride. She wasn't prepared to leave her family in Sylva, North Carolina, and encouraged him to stay there with her.

Ralph was devastated. After a teary farewell, he continued on to Boston, where he persuaded his younger brother Earle and their mother, Gertrude, and much younger brother, Bruce, to go back to Bella Coola with him. He found a place for Gertrude and Bruce to live, and Ralph helped Earle establish his own pre-emption a few miles south of Lonesome Lake.

This should have been a happy time for Ralph, surrounded by family, but his bubble burst when he got a letter from Helen Cathie telling him she was about to get married. Alone at the lake, he was depressed and angry.

Rather than brood about something he couldn't change, Ralph headed to Vancouver to join the war effort and tried to enlist in the Canadian Air Force. He had long had dreams to be a pilot. Sadly Ralph failed the physical examination because he was short-sighted in one eye. Determined to get into the air war, he crossed the border into Washington State and applied at the US Air Force recruiting office. Again he was rejected, this time because he didn't have enough formal education.

Finally Ralph got accepted by the US Army Signal Corps as a telegrapher, and in the summer of 1917 he headed off to war in Europe. He survived the ordeal dodging bullets and dysentery.

"I bellied my way through mud and dead bodies to set up wireless equipment while shells burst all around me," he said. "I began to think that facing grizzly bears in British Columbia was not such a dangerous piece of work."[4]

After the armistice declaring an end to the "war to end all wars" was signed in 1918, death still stalked the soldiers. Many died from the Spanish flu that had become a worldwide pandemic. Ralph was impressed when a German farm wife applied homespun medicine to save the lives of flu victims. When he was discharged at Fort Lawton, Washington, in 1919, he climbed aboard a train to Vancouver, where he bought a suit to replace his uniform.

---

4   Edwards and Gould, *Ralph Edwards*, 86.

"With some of my discharge pay I bought a new rifle and a one-way ticket to Bella Coola. It would be a long, long time before I would leave the valley again."[5]

In September 1919 Ralph stepped off the Union Steamship boat onto the wharf in Bella Coola. Compared with the hell of war, his wilderness paradise populated by grizzly bears, cougars and wolves was a welcome respite. He was eager to resume his pioneering at the Birches. Maxie Heckman, the one-armed trapper at Atnarko, welcomed Ralph into his stopping house beside the river, halfway between the end of the road at Firvale and Ralph's homestead on Lonesome Lake. A night at Maxie's was the surest way to catch up on the latest news about men in the valley who had gone to war and never returned.

Accommodation at Maxie's hadn't changed much in the two years Ralph had been away. The smoke-begrimed guest room in the attic with two double beds and blankets infused with sweat and smoke were still the same. Lodgers dutifully hung the blankets over a rafter to dissuade mice from colonizing the bedding after their night's rest.

Maxie's guest house offered Ralph a warm place to stay during his comings and goings to get his mail and supplies. Upstream from Maxie's place, the rugged trail followed the Atnarko River to Stillwater Lake and beyond there to the outflow of Lonesome Lake. From there the trail crossed the river and followed the west side of Lonesome Lake to the Birches at the far end of the lake.

When he had supplies to bring in, Ralph boated or rafted them up the lake. In winter he walked on the ice. Upon his return after a two-year absence, Ralph couldn't find the dugout he had cached at the outflow of Lonesome Lake, so he hastily built a raft and fashioned a set of oars to propel it. As he proceeded down the lake, he shot three black bears and loaded the carcasses aboard his makeshift craft. It was all he could do to keep afloat as he neared home, but it meant fresh meat, lard for cooking, grease for his boots and hides to sell to the fur buyer for cash income.

Nobody had been near his homestead since he had been gone, but Mother Nature hadn't wasted any time attempting to reclaim his civilizing efforts. Second-growth trees had invaded the 6 acres (2.4 hectares) of fields and pasture he had cleared, and his garden was a riot of weeds. Some of the fruit trees in his orchard had perished from frost or from animals chewing the trunks, but Ralph was pleased that his wilderness abode had stayed intact during his absence.

His house built beside a babbling creek was still sound, and he quickly resumed his efforts to clear more land and get his traps ready for winter. A week after Ralph returned, his brother Earle arrived after being discharged

---

5   Edwards and Gould, *Ralph Edwards*, 89.

from the Canadian Army. Earle had spent one year with Ralph at Lonesome Lake prior to the war, and he too was eager to pick up where he had left off.

Earle was new to trapping, so Ralph showed him how to set traps and snares to catch the fur-bearers. Trapping was the mainstay of the backwoods economy, and Earle established his own trapping area in the rugged headwaters of the Talchako River west of Ralph's domain. The region was well stocked with beaver, mink, marten and muskrat, and by spring both men had reaped bountiful harvests.

By the summer of 1920 Ralph had awoken to the fact that he needed a horse to help pack in supplies and work the ground on his homestead. He hiked up the Charlotte Lake trail to the Chilcotin Plateau and bought a young colt from Tom Engebretson at Towdystan for ten dollars. He named the horse Ginty, and the faithful steed became one of the most important assets on the farm for many years to come. The following year Ralph added two more horses, Queenie and Old Blue, to his pack string, and this enabled him to haul in farm equipment and supplies from the end of the road at Stuie.

After trapping with Ralph for a couple of seasons and trying his hand at fishing, Earle left the country for Oregon. Ralph turned thirty years old in 1921 and had gotten over his broken heart from Helen Cathie's rejection several years earlier. In his solitude he staved off loneliness by putting in eighteen-hour days building his homestead. His horses and dog provided companionship, but he badly wanted a wife to fill the void in his personal life. This was easier said than done.

George Powers of Charlotte Lake and George Turner of Kleena Kleene had taken Indigenous women for their partners, but Ralph was determined to have a spouse from his own ethnic background. Isabel Edwards, who married Ralph's brother Earle in 1926, said that settler women inhabited only the lower twenty-eight miles (forty-five kilometres) of the valley.

"It was a bachelor's world beyond the Seventh Day Adventist colony at Firvale," she wrote in her 1980 memoir, *Ruffles on My Longjohns*.[6] "All the settlers along the Atnarko were young men in their prime, eager to carve a home for themselves out of the dense forests."

She mentioned the names of several single men who had come to trap and open up the Atnarko Valley frontier: Gyllenspetz, a Swedish aristocrat; Creswell, an Oxford University–educated remittance man; brothers Maxie and Lou Heckman, miners from Switzerland; George Young, a miner from England; Mark Marvin, rumoured to have been an English diplomat; the Chadwell brothers from Oregon; and the Ratcliffs, Milo, Frank, Walter and Johnny, also from Oregon.

---

6   Isabel Edwards, *Ruffles on My Longjohns* (Surrey, BC: Hancock House, 1980), 57.

Some of these bachelors, like the Ratcliffs, eventually got married and moved farther down the valley, returning for only a couple of months each winter to run their traplines.

On his infrequent forays into civilization to get his mail and supplies, Ralph started spending more and more time at Firvale. Ostensibly he came to see the Ratcliffs, but he would also visit the Hobers, a Seventh-day Adventist family with a large number of children. Their oldest daughter, eighteen-year-old Ethel, had caught Ralph's eye.

"John Hober reminded me of my relatives, and we spent long hours talking about religion and politics," Ralph said in his memoir.[7]

He tried to convince himself he was taking the long trips into Firvale to talk religion with John Hober, but the real reason was Ethel. Courting Ethel was a challenge. There was a thirteen-year age difference between the two, and the Hobers didn't make it easy. They were very strict and would not permit any parlour romancing or hand holding in their domain.

So in October 1922 Ralph invited Mrs. Hober and Ethel to come and spend a week with him at the Birches. They willingly agreed, and with Ralph leading the way they set out on the thirty-mile (fifty-kilometre) journey from Firvale on horseback. Both Ethel and her mother were impressed by the home Ralph had crafted in the wilderness. Ethel and Ralph got better acquainted, taking long walks together and going on short hunting and trapping forays. Ralph was impressed by Ethel's ability to handle the wild and her capacity to manage the horses. Both mother and daughter loved Lonesome Lake and its enchanted view. As the week drew to a close, Ralph mustered up the courage to ask Ethel to marry him.

"As we tramped back along the treacherous trail to Firvale, Ethel and I had somehow become engaged."[8]

They were married the following summer, on August 23, 1923, at the Hober home. Everyone within miles of Firvale came to wish them well. Within a few hours of their simple Adventist ceremony, Ralph and Ethel headed up to the trail on horseback. Lonesome Lake wasn't going to be lonesome anymore.

A few wildflowers in jam jars, handmade curtains covering the windows, a tablecloth sewn from sacking, a chair angled in a certain way: these all reflected the new feminine touch Ethel Hober brought to Ralph Edwards's bachelor existence on Lonesome Lake. So began their married life.

Their immediate task was to prepare for winter. This included hauling in supplies and cutting hay for livestock. Besides Ralph's string of

---

7   Edwards and Gould, *Ralph Edwards*, 104.
8   Edwards and Gould, *Ralph Edwards*, 106.

Ralph and Ethel Edwards' wedding in 1923. Left to right, standing: Laura Hober, Ralph Edwards, Ruth Hober, John Hober, Sarah Hober, the pastor. Front row: Ethel Edwards and her mother, Ida Mae Hober. Photo published on page 146 in Trudy Turner's memoir, *Packtrains & Airplanes: Memories of Lonesome Lake* [Hancock House, 2012]

horses, they now owned an Ayrshire milk cow, Maybelle, that Ethel's family had given them for a wedding gift. They eventually added a bull, and over the years their cattle herd grew to fourteen animals.

Ethel was accustomed to the rigours of homestead life, but at nineteen years old, she had never experienced the profound solitude of being alone in the wilderness before. When Ralph was off trapping, it was up to her to keep the home fires burning. To ease her angst, Ralph made an effort to be punctual.

"I always made a point of getting back on the day or night I told her to expect me," Ralph told Ed Gould.[9]

Sometimes the weather or circumstances prevented this from happening, but for the most part he would show up as promised. For her part, Ethel quelled the loneliness with a busy routine of sewing, weaving, baking and canning. She also fed the animals, milked the cow and sawed and chopped firewood.

Ethel took delight in accompanying Ralph when he trekked out to Atnarko to get the mail or supplies. She would travel as far as the

Isabel Edwards milking her milk cow, Modesta, "the one animal I loved unreservedly," she writes on p. 136 in her memoir, *Ruffles on my Longjohns.* [Hancock House 1980]

Stillwater, where their horses were pastured for the winter, and stay there in the Ratcliff cabin until Ralph returned from Stuie. Ethel's solitude at the Birches was short-lived. As spring melted the ice on Lonesome Lake, she realized she was pregnant. On September 24, 1924, she gave birth to their first child, Stanley Bruce, at the hospital in Bella Coola.

9   Edwards and Gould, *Ralph Edwards*, 113.

The Edwards family home at the Birches. Photo published on page 147 in Trudy Turner's memoir, *Packtrains & Airplanes: Memories of Lonesome Lake* [Hancock House, 2012]

The birth went smoothly, but the journey from Lonesome Lake to Bella Coola and home again was challenging. They hiked the trail to Stillwater, where they caught two horses and spent the night. The next day at dawn they set out for Firvale on horseback. When they arrived, Ethel's dad insisted they take the horse-drawn wagon to Bella Coola. Unfortunately the jolting of the wagon ride was more uncomfortable than riding by saddle horse.

After the birth, the new family stayed for a couple of months at the Hober farm in Firvale, and this almost led to their undoing. The weather was cold and blowing snow when they finally departed for home in November, and two-month-old Stanley almost suffocated from being over-bundled against the inclement weather. Chalk it up to the new parents' inexperience. Fortunately Stanley survived and they got home safely.

With the arrival of Stanley Bruce, Ralph felt the urgency for a steady income to support his family. Their primary source of cash came from the trapline. In his ingenious way Ralph concluded that farming fur might generate a more reliable source of revenue and inflict less pain on the fur-bearers he caught in the wild. It would also mean not leaving his wife and son alone for days at a time while he checked his traps.

First he tried farming beaver by containing the animals in a large enclosure and feeding them with aspens that grew prolifically along the lakeshore. It worked well except the animals were continually breaking out of their pen by chewing holes in the fencing.

Next he tried farming mink and marten, feeding them horsemeat he purchased from Hunlin, a Tŝilhqot'in man from Nimpo Lake. To render the

Ralph Edwards plowing at the Birches in the late 1940s. Photo published on page 153 in Trudy Turner's memoir, *Packtrains & Airplanes: Memories of Lonesome Lake* [Hancock House, 2012]

horsemeat into edible portions, he ground it up with squawfish, now known as northern pike-minnow, taken from the river and lake, and with carrots from his garden. To ease the strenuous workload of grinding that much feed, Ralph devised a water wheel that he later converted to power a sawmill, and then to generate electricity.

Ralph decided that constantly repairing the beaver fencing required too much time and trouble, and farming marten was too precarious because the males and females would rather fight than procreate. Mink farming, however, proved more satisfactory, until the Great Depression sent fur prices plummeting and it was no longer profitable.

It was a visit from K.B. (Kennon Beverly) Moore, a rancher from Tatlayoko Lake, in 1926 that introduced a brand new perspective to Ralph and Ethel's way of life. K.B. arrived with some American bear hunters and asked Ralph and Walter Ratcliff to guide them in the Atnarko Valley. One of the hunters was John P. Holman of Connecticut, a member of the Audubon Society. Holman asked many questions about the trumpeter swans that wintered at Lonesome Lake, and on his way home he contacted the chief migratory bird warden for British Columbia, J.A. Munro. Munro wrote to Ralph and Ethel asking about the size of the flock and persuaded the Edwardses to start keeping careful records of all swans they saw in winter until the birds left in the spring.

Ralph had been aware of the swans since his first winter at Lonesome Lake in 1913. That year Frank Ratcliff shot a swan, and he and Ralph pan-fried it like a steak and found it good tasting and filling. At that time there was no law prohibiting the shooting of trumpeter swans, nor was it widely known that they were an endangered species.

These magnificent birds with a wingspan of up to 8 feet (2.5 metres) once inhabited all of Canada from northern Quebec to the Pacific coast. Then during the nineteenth century swan skins became a coveted commodity of the fur trade. Swan down was popular for muffs and bedding, and the quills were prized for pens. Between 1853 and 1877 the Hudson's Bay Company sold 17,671 swan skins in London, and in 1828 alone, the company sold 347,298 goose, swan and eagle quills for pens. In 1912, the year Ralph Edwards arrived in the Bella Coola Valley, prominent ornithologist Edward H. Forbush warned that the extinction of trumpeter swans was imminent.[10]

Four years later it was estimated there were only a hundred trumpeters left in the world, and a third of those wintered in the Atnarko Valley at Lonesome Lake. There, springs fed sections of the river and kept it free of ice so they could feed.

During the winter of 1932–33, Mother Nature dealt a severe blow that nearly eradicated the great birds wintering in the Atnarko. A three-day downpour of rain triggered landslides that dammed up parts of the river, which led to widespread flooding. Then a sudden drop in temperature caused the high water to freeze over the swans' feeding grounds. Ralph counted eleven dead swans on one of his rounds running his trapline. By spring the flock was reduced to nineteen birds.

In his annual report to J.A. Munro, Ralph suggested that feeding the swans during the hard part of winter might help them survive. Munro agreed and gave Ralph the authority to purchase twenty-five dollars' worth of barley to start a feeding program. In 1932 this translated to 800 pounds (360 kilograms) of barley in 100-pound (45-kilogram) sacks. It was up to Ralph on his own dime and muscle to haul the feed into Lonesome Lake by pack horse from the end of the vehicle road at Belarko, near the confluence of the Atnarko and Talchako Rivers. For best results they learned by trial and error to first soak the grain overnight before depositing it in about 2 feet (60 centimetres) of water, half a pound (230 grams) of grain per bird per day.

Meanwhile the Edwards family continued to expand. In July 1927 Ethel gave birth to a second son, John. This time the birthing occurred at home with the aid of a visiting doctor. Two years later, on March 30, 1929, their daughter, Trudy, was born, with Ralph alone performing the midwifery duties. That completed their family as they continued their unique existence in the Lonesome Lake wilderness.

After the stock market crashed on Wall Street in New York City on October 29, 1929, the global economic meltdown was so severe that this day became known as Black Tuesday. It marked the start of the Great Depression that would endure for a decade and affect all Western industrialized countries.

In the Bella Coola Valley, where money was scarce anyway, the world's financial downturn was somewhat muted. At least at first. For the Edwards family, living isolated at Lonesome Lake, the woes of Wall Street were so far from their world that they hardly paid attention to it. In the summer of 1929 they'd had a bountiful harvest in their garden. Ethel had preserved five hundred jars of vegetables, fruit and meat and stored

---

10   Edwards and Gould, *Ralph Edwards*, 158.

The west end of the henhouse that the family moved into after a fire destroyed their home in 1929. Photo published on page 147 in Trudy Turner's memoir, *Packtrains & Airplanes: Memories of Lonesome Lake* [Hancock House, 2012]

them in the root cellar beneath their log house. Also filling the larder were a hundred pounds (forty-five kilograms) of cooking onions and six sacks of potatoes.

In late October Ralph was in the garden digging the last of their spuds when he heard five-year-old Stanley yelling from the house. He didn't pay much attetion to it at first because Stanley was always yelling about something. Then Ralph noticed a big column of smoke rising from where the house stood in a big clump of birch trees. He dropped his garden fork and ran. As he approached he could hear bullets exploding and ricocheting in all directions from his loaded rifles inside the house. The place was an inferno when he got there. Ralph kicked in the front door and was met by a wall of flame. Ethel and the children were safely distanced in the field on the opposite side of the house. Before she had retreated with the children, Ethel had thrown an armful of blankets and the family cash box outside. Everything else, including the year's supply of food carefully preserved for the winter, clothes, bedding, tools and the marvellous library of books Ralph had been collecting since his arrival seventeen years earlier, was destroyed. The sound of sealers popping and the aroma of vegetables and meat cooking only served to increase the family's hunger pangs.

"It drew our attention to the fact that we were stuck in the wilderness without food, clothing or defense against wild animals," Ralph said.[11]

When Ethel asked what they were going to do next, Ralph responded that they still had spuds and root crops in the garden and a fatted calf in the pasture. Within an hour he slaughtered the calf and they feasted on veal and potatoes served around the ashes of their dream home. The children were five years, three years, and six months old when they moved into the small, 10-by-14-foot (3-by-4.25-metre), dirt-floor trap cabin Ralph had constructed in 1913 with Frank Ratcliff.

Fortunately they had a cache of blankets and old clothing at their stopover cabin at Stillwater Lake, which Ralph retrieved the next day. Then at first light the following day, he headed out to Atnarko to place

---

11   Edwards and Gould, *Ralph Edwards*, 142.

a food order over the phone to Bella Coola. Store owner Andy Christensen generously extended them credit. When his order of food and
supplies arrived by team and wagon the next day at Atnarko, Ralph was
overwhelmed by the kindness of his Bella Coola neighbours. Word had
got out about their plight, and people responded quickly.

Despite the economic crunch gripping the world, people in the valley pooled their resources and donated a hundred dollars in cash along
with blankets, clothing and household items for the destitute family.
Ralph loaded his two pack horses, Ginty and Blue, with the urgently
needed food and supplies and headed for home. One gift he received was
a new suit marked, "From a good friend." He never discovered who that
good friend was, but the donor knew his size.

Ralph's father also sent him a hundred dollars, and two hunters
Ralph had guided sent a generous supply of books. Books were particularly meaningful as tools of education for the children and as sources of
knowledge to survive in the bush.

"We were all voracious readers," Ralph said. "The books sent by the
hunters would be a God-send in the long hours we would be spending
in the little trappers cabin."[12]

The winter of 1929–30 continued to hand out its challenges. In January Ralph had a near-death encounter with his Holstein bull when he
headed out to bring the cattle home from winter grazing up the Atnarko
River. The three-year-old bull took exception to having a rope placed
over his horns and attacked Ralph with a vengeance that left him bruised
and bleeding with an assortment of broken ribs. Ralph was forced to shoot
his valuable breeding bull, which the family could ill afford to replace, as he
staggered to the nearest trapline cabin to recover. He arrived home late the
next day without his herd of bovines and managed to survive thanks to
Ethel's nursing and knowledge of backwoods medicine. On top of that,
she had three small children to look after in their cramped living quarters, along with all the chores required on the homestead, and she took
it all in stride.

It took Ralph months to recover. After a week of Ethel's treatment he
was strong enough to trek up the valley to bring their milk cow and calf
home, but trouble still had a few more surprises in store. One night during
a big windstorm, two big trees toppled onto the barn, collapsing the roof
and bulging out the log sides of the structure. Ralph wondered what else
could go wrong, and he didn't have to wait long to find out. When he
picked up his fur cheque at the post office in the spring, he was devastated to discover that the prices had fallen to a tenth of their previous value.
Mink, the staple of their family income, normally brought twenty to thirty dollars apiece. Now they yielded only three dollars or less.

---

12   Edwards and Gould, *Ralph Edwards*, 144.

"The Great Depression had hit Lonesome Lake at last," Ralph mused. "There was no escaping its insidious grasp."[13]

During the winter Ralph and Ethel picked out a new spot to rebuild their house. Then Ralph realized that the half-finished chicken house he had started building before the fire would make an adequate family dwelling. It was a solid 10-by-24-foot (3-by-7.3-metre) structure, and it would allow them to move out of the cramped trap cabin much sooner. He pitched the idea to Ethel and she agreed. So the chickens remained where they were, and the partially completed henhouse was redesigned for the family. It was supposed to be only a temporary shelter until their planned new house got built. But that never happened. They remained in the chicken house the rest of their lives, adding on to it as needed.

Their new quarters were still unfinished when they moved into them at the end of March, but they were a welcome reprieve after enduring six months in the rustic trap cabin. The barn was repaired, and Ralph fashioned new furniture out of birchwood to replace the tables and chairs that had burned up in the fire. As the family embraced a new growing season, Ethel began canning vegetables, meat and salmon in brand new sealers brought in from Bella Coola. This time a root cellar was constructed away from the house to thwart any further losses of their food supply should fire occur again.

The boys were getting old enough to lend a hand in the fields, and by the fall of 1930, six-year-old Stanley was ready for school. The nearest school was a two-day journey away, so Ralph and Ethel educated him at home. They used Stanley's natural curiosity to propel his learning. When his questions stumped his parents, Ralph would send for more and more books to rebuild the library that had been destroyed by the fire.

Book learning was dull compared with the rigours of daily outdoor life, so to help them organize a structured system of lessons, the Edwardses enrolled the children in the public correspondence program as well. Ralph cleverly introduced practical mathematical problems around the homestead for the children to figure out to bring the book learning alive. How many board feet of lumber would be needed for the new barn? How many logs would be required for the new bull pen?

As the kids got older, the school problems got more complex. Figuring out the mathematical aspects of setting up a new generator was one challenge. How much horsepower would be required to lift a stump ten feet (three metres) in the air? Ralph also got books on mineralogy and set up a homemade chemical laboratory so Stanley and the younger kids could make acid tests of rocks, or manufacture tanning extract from hemlock bark.

---

13   Edwards and Gould, *Ralph Edwards*, 156.

The growing collection of high school and university textbooks served to educate Ethel and Ralph as much as it did the children. In time their curiosity would push them into another frontier of learning: how to build an airplane in the wilderness and learn to fly.

When the two boys reached eleven years old, they each built their own log cabin and used it as their own personal domain and sleeping quarters. Trudy started correspondence classes at age eleven and went through grades four and five in the first year, then did one grade a year after that until her formal schooling ended at grade nine.

John, six, and Trudy, four, warming up in the sun at Lonesome Lake. Photo published on page 149 in Trudy Turner's memoir, *Packtrains & Airplanes: Memories of Lonesome Lake* [Hancock House, 2012]

"I grew up with books and truly cannot remember ever being unable to read," she wrote in her 1977 memoir, *Fogswamp: Living with Swans in the Wilderness*.[14]

It was actually the queries from the children that helped expand the family's knowledge base. They acquired a set of encyclopedias to help answer the children's questions, and Ralph ordered how-to books on various subjects. Every mail day, more and more books arrived. Trudy said there were hundreds of books on the shelves at the Birches.

"Every cent my father could spare was always spent on books."[15]

Trudy had a greater affinity for farming and life on the homestead at Lonesome Lake than her two brothers did. Stanley left home at seventeen to seek his fortune at the pulp mill in Ocean Falls. Two years after that, John set out on his own when he was sixteen. By the time Trudy was thirteen years old she was Ralph and Ethel's "right hand man."[16]

One of Trudy's chores since early childhood was feeding the trumpeter swans that the Edwards family brought back from the brink of extinction. Later, as she got older, the stipend paid by the Canadian Wildlife Service became her personal source of income. The big birds' ability to spread their expansive wingspans and take off inspired both Trudy and Ralph to become pilots. If they can do it, why can't we?

---

14   Trudy Turner and Ruth M. McVeigh, *Fogswamp: Living with Swans in the Wilderness* (Surrey, BC: Hancock House, 1977), 15.

15   Turner and McVeigh, *Fogswamp*, 15–16.

16   Turner and McVeigh, *Fogswamp*, 14.

There was a practical reason for this as well. Every year Ralph and Trudy packed hundreds of pounds of grain with their horses to feed the swans. This meant many trips over the rugged trail from the end of the road at Atnarko. How much easier would it be to fly the grain into Lonesome Lake? There were other considerations too, such as the ease of delivering farm products to customers in the surrounding area.

Buying an airplane during the Great Depression years was out of the question, so Ralph decided to build one. He subscribed to aviation magazines and bought several books on aviation design. He quickly realized that his ignorance of mathematics stood in his way, so he mailed away for home study books on quadratic equations, algebra, trigonometry, geometry, logarithms and everything connected to aeronautics. Soon he could understand what he was reading.

At the end of the Second World War there was a renewed interest in flying and an abundance of old airplanes and parts that were selling cheaply. Ralph bought an eighty-horsepower motor and ordered a propeller, bolts, aircraft dope, fabric and fuselage parts from Winnipeg and had them shipped by boat to Bella Coola. He transported them from the end of the road at Atnarko to Lonesome Lake with his horses. The engine weighed 180 pounds (82 kilograms), so he built a travois and coaxed one of his faithful animals over the rugged trail, several times averting near tragedy.

At the ranch, Ralph set the engine up on two upright poles. He filled the sump with oil and turned the engine over. He said it ran like a new watch.[17] That's where the airplane motor remained for ten years as Ralph contemplated how to build a fuselage and wings around it.

It was pilot Johnny Hatch who persuaded Ralph not to go ahead with building the plane. Johnny stopped in to visit after delivering a load of grain for the swans.

"The Department of Transport would never let you fly your home-made plane," he advised Ralph. "Even if they did, it could take years before they would certify it."[18]

He urged Ralph to buy a good used plane. Ralph was no spring chicken. He turned sixty in 1951, and time was running out for him to get his wings.

Trudy shared her father's enthusiasm for flying and purchasing an airplane. By pooling their resources they figured they had enough. Ralph had savings from guiding and trapping, and Trudy had saved most of her income from feeding the swans.

---

17 Edwards and Gould, *Ralph Edwards*, 201.

18 Edwards and Gould, *Ralph Edwards*, 204.

Ralph Edwards standing in the hangar at Lonesome Lake built from timbers cut on his hand-built, water-powered sawmill. Photo published on page 196 in *Ralph Edwards of Lonesome Lake* [Hancock House, 1979]

Trudy was twenty-four years old when she headed off to Vancouver in April 1953 to learn to fly and buy an airplane. This was her first trip out of the wilderness to the big city, and thanks to the kindness of Johnny Hatch and his family, she averted any major culture shock.

"The Hatch family opened their home to Mom," Trudy's daughter Susan Turner told me. "Johnny dutifully drove her to Vancouver's Sea Island airport for her flying instructions. She spent all her non-flying time on the Hatches' farm in the Fraser Valley, so hardly saw the city. Mom was a keen learner and got her pilot's licence quite easily. She had amassed considerable book knowledge from reading books and magazines on aviation, so she was well prepared."

The previous winter, Trudy and Ralph had built a hangar on the ice of Lonesome Lake next to the shore. The 30-by-40-foot (9-by-12-metre) structure was designed to settle into the shallows of the lagoon at one end and rest on the shore at the other, once the ice melted in the spring. It was a complicated engineering feat. The goal was to end up with a level floor inside the hangar once the 40-foot (12-metre) sill log settled in the mud.

Ralph drilled through the ice to determine the depth of the water and then built the hangar accordingly. Like many other projects on the homestead, the 25-foot-high (7.5-metre-high) hangar turned out the way it was intended, and miraculously the floor was level. While Trudy was away in Vancouver, Ralph added shakes to the roof of the hangar and constructed a sloping entrance deck for the plane.

Once Trudy got her pilot's licence, her next task was to find an appropriate aircraft. A family friend, Roy Moulton, a pilot for Pacific

Trudy Edwards (Turner) with the Taylorcraft airplane she purchased with her father, Ralph Edwards, in 1953. This was the cover photo on Trudy's memoir *Packtrains & Airplanes: Memories of Lonesome Lake* [Hancock House, 2012]

Western Airlines in Vancouver, flew her to Grand Coulee Dam in Washington State, where a 65 hp on floats was available. Trudy bought the plane for $2,500, and Roy flew the two-seater registered with the call sign CF-HEO back to Vancouver because Trudy still had to get certified to land and take off from water. She earned her float plane endorsement in short order and was ready to return home. On July 8, 1953, Trudy piloted

CF-HEO up the coast to Bella Coola, and around five in the afternoon she landed at Lonesome Lake and taxied up to the newly completed hangar at the Birches.

Once Trudy was back home with the plane, the Edwards family started to realize their dream of getting farm products to market. Trudy flew her father to Charlotte and Nimpo Lakes to explore the possibilities. The fish camps and lodges were eager to have fresh produce and dairy products.

Ralph Edwards at Bella Coola in 1956 with his Taylorcraft airplane. Cliff Kopas photo, published on page 74 in Leslie Kopas's self-published book *Bella Coola Country*. Cliff Kopas photo courtesy Leslie Kopas

Then they flew out to isolated logging camps on the coast and found the same eager appetite for their goods. In his 1979 memoir, Ralph described his first flight with Trudy:

"We flew up out of the valley and in less than forty minutes we were at Charlotte Lake where there were two big fish camps. We asked the operators if they would like us to fly in fresh vegetables every week or two. Does a duck swim? Of course they would. No luxuries like fresh produce had been available before."[19]

That summer and fall of 1953, Trudy logged more than two hundred hours airfreighting fresh milk, cream, butter, eggs, lettuce, radishes, tomatoes, corn, beans, carrots, potatoes, strawberries and whatever fruits were in season.

In the spring of 1954, at sixty-two years old, Ralph went to Vancouver to get his pilot's licence. It was his first visit to the city since his return from the First World War in 1919. When he presented himself for a pre-flight medical exam, the doctor asked if he wasn't a bit too old to fly. Despite being nervous, Ralph had the blood pressure of a twenty-eight-year-old, and he passed with flying colours.

After a month of flight instruction, Ralph got his water endorsement qualifying him to fly a float plane. Back home he learned to operate the Taylorcraft under Trudy's careful tutelage. For weeks he spent an hour a day perfecting his landings and takeoffs and accompanied Trudy on her flights to deliver produce to the various fish camps. Soon he was able to take flights on his own.

---

19   Edwards and Gould, *Ralph Edwards*, 208.

Sharing the use of the plane with her domineering father proved difficult for Trudy.

"I never flew her after 1958 because it became too difficult to plan the sharing of the schedule with my father," she wrote in her memoir.[20]

By that time, Trudy had met her husband, Jack Turner, and was developing her own farm and ranch a few miles away from her parents' homestead.

Just as horses had proved essential to homesteading at Lonesome Lake in the 1920s, the Taylorcraft became equally vital to the Edwards family more than three decades later. Soon they had a hard time imagining life without it. Besides delivering fresh produce and farm products to customers on the Chilcotin Plateau and coastal logging and fishing camps, Ralph and Trudy used the plane to haul food and supplies into Lonesome Lake. This included grain for the swans, livestock—calves, young horses and chickens were stuffed into the cockpit—and even a tractor that was taken apart and flown in and reassembled at Lonesome Lake.

Trudy married Jack Turner in January 1957, and two years later their daughter Susan was born. The Turners built their own farm along the upper Atnarko River, three miles (five kilometres) upstream from Lonesome Lake, and named it Arbordale.

Trudy originally called the place Fogswamp Farm, reflecting an earlier tragedy in which she had felled a tree on her beloved dog, killing it instantly. In her remorse she gave it the most dreary and mournful name she could think of. When Jack arrived, they started creating happy memories. Thus was born Arbordale.

Ralph had his share of adventures and near tragedies during his thirteen-year flying career. After several hard landings and other scrapes in the rugged landscape, Ralph flew the Taylorcraft to Vancouver to repair a bent cross member on the bottom of the fuselage. When mechanic Gordy Peters examined the plane, he had bad news.

"Look at this," he said to Ralph, poking his pocket knife through the corroded steel tubing in several places. "You will need $1,800 for a new fuselage."[21]

This was money Ralph didn't have, but he gave the go-ahead for the repairs and returned to Lonesome Lake. Ralph and Ethel decided to mortgage their cattle herd to pay the bill.

When he got word that repairs to the Taylorcraft were complete, Ralph took the steamship to Vancouver and was shocked to find that the rebuild job exceeded the work they had agreed upon. A radio had been installed as well as new upholstery, a windscreen and a door. No way

---

20   Turner and McVeigh, *Fogswamp*, 18.

21   Edwards and Gould, *Ralph Edwards*, 236.

could Ralph afford the $5,000 bill.

Then, in front of a group of aviators who had gathered for the occasion, pilot Roy Moulton tore up the stack of invoices, and his friends all applauded.

"The expenses are all taken care of," Roy announced to a surprised Ralph Edwards. "The guys here all donated their services, and Grant McConachie and other airlines brass threw in a few hundred bucks to pay for the radio, seat and door and other stuff."[22]

Ralph was overwhelmed. With a radio installed for the first time, he felt he had joined the modern age.

Ralph turned sixty-nine in 1960, and the publicity generated by Leland Stowe's 1957 book *Crusoe of Lonesome Lake* earned him a surprise television appearance in Hollywood the following year. This brought additional international fame to the reclusive family of Lonesome Lake.

Every mail day there was a gunny sack of correspondence from people curious about escaping to the wilds of British Columbia. On top of that, more and more tourist lodges and cottages were getting established on lakes in the West Chilcotin.

"Our magnificent isolation was ending," Ralph observed. "Hardly a day went by without planes circling overhead. I was beginning to feel hemmed in."[23]

Ralph approached Ethel about the idea of selling out and starting again somewhere else, but Ethel was determined to remain with her beloved cattle and the home she had known since she was nineteen years old. She said he could do what he wanted, but she wasn't leaving.

Ralph put the Lonesome Lake property up for sale and set out in the Taylorcraft in search of a new home. With provisions and extra gas, he headed north to Kispiox and then on to Dease Lake. Landing on various lakes, he made inquiries about available land and was told that nothing was available. This was the same message he had received fifty years earlier when he first arrived in Bella Coola.

Undaunted, Ralph flew to the Yukon, where the government agent in Whitehorse said there were only two arable farms in the whole territory. He said dozens of attempts had been made to establish others but all had failed.

Ralph turned seventy before he arrived back at Lonesome Lake to put up the hay for the winter. In October he headed out again, this time for Haida Gwaii and Prince Rupert. When he landed in the isolated community of Oona River on Porcher Island at the mouth of the Skeena River, he figured he found what he was looking for.

---

22   Edwards and Gould, *Ralph Edwards*, 237–38.

23   Edwards and Gould, *Ralph Edwards*, 270.

Ralph Edwards at Oona River. Page 188 in *Ralph Edwards of Lonesome Lake.* [Hancock House, 1979]

On a hunch that Ethel would go for this remote settlement twenty-six miles (forty-two kilometres) south of Prince Rupert, Ralph bought a house there with a big garden, running water and inside plumbing.

"The price was right so I decided to buy it. I hoped Ethel would like it too."[24]

But Ethel wasn't impressed. Her heart wasn't won, and she wanted to remain at Lonesome Lake close to their daughter Trudy, son-in-law Jack and three-year-old granddaughter Susan, only three miles (five kilometres) away.

Ralph felt stunned and hurt that his wife wouldn't simply follow his lead, but he made his move to Oona River anyway. He settled into community life and became a local celebrity as the Crusoe of Lonesome Lake, and he bought a gillnetter and went commercial fishing.

Ralph still loved Ethel and would fly home to Lonesome Lake every month or so to deliver the mail and bring in supplies. When he sold the Lonesome Lake homestead to Americans from California, Ralph made the stipulation that Ethel could remain there the rest of her life. Their son Stanley moved back home to help his mother.

On July 21, 1967, life changed forever for Ralph Edwards, who was now seventy-six years old. He was flying the Taylorcraft up the Bella Coola Valley to Lonesome Lake, attempting to gain altitude to cross 8,747-foot (2,666-metre) Defiance Mountain and 8,200-foot (2,500-metre) Stupendous Mountain, when his plane lost power. Fortunately he had enough altitude to swing around and make an emergency landing in the Bella Coola River. He was twelve miles (nineteen kilometres) upstream from the Wilderness Airlines seaplane base at the mouth of the river when he touched down on the turbulent waters. He managed to poke his way downriver through the "floating impedimenta,"[25] gravel bars and logjams despite one of his floats starting to take on water.

---

24 Edwards and Gould, *Ralph Edwards,* 277.

25 Edwards and Gould, *Ralph Edwards,* 12.

Gideon Schuetze rescues Ralph Edwards from his overturned Taylorcraft in the Bella Coola River in front of the Wilderness Airlines float plane base in Bella Coola. Cliff Kopas photo courtesy Leslie Kopas

He said the plane was starting to "droop like a sad seagull"[26] when he finally drifted abreast of the Wilderness Airlines float plane dock near the mouth of the river, but the Taylorcraft didn't have enough engine power to cross through the current. A rescue boat came to help just as Ralph stepped off the pontoon into the river. Then a sudden gust of wind grabbed the wing of the listing plane and flipped it upside down in the shallow water. The plane came to rest against the rocks of a small islet in the river, and Ralph's flying days were done.

For the last decade of his life, Ralph used commercial aircraft to commute between Oona River and Lonesome Lake to visit Ethel. He had one final hurrah in 1972 when he was invited to Ottawa to receive the Order of Canada for his work preserving the trumpeter swans. He insisted that Ethel be invited too, and after some persuasion she agreed to

Ralph Edwards at his Oona River home. Page 200 in *Ralph Edwards of Lonesome Lake*. [Hancock House, 1979]

26   Edwards and Gould, *Ralph Edwards*, 12.

accompany him. Governor General Roland Michener bestowed the Medal of Service, and they were introduced to Prime Minister Pierre Elliott Trudeau.

Five years later Ralph Edwards died in Prince Rupert at the age of eighty-six. Ethel died two years after that in Bella Coola. Their children, Stanley, John and Trudy, continued to maintain the family legacy at Lonesome Lake for many years afterwards. Trudy and Jack remained at Arbordale until 1989, when they sold out and moved to the sunny Salloomt near Hagensborg in the Bella Coola Valley.

Stanley made his home at Stillwater Lake and was always quite noticeable in his signature yellow hard hat, rubber gumboots and long white beard when he made shopping visits to Hagensborg and Bella Coola. He later died at his cabin on the Stillwater.

John rented canoes to tourists for many years on Turner Lake, where he was famous for his Wilderness Bakery. Fresh cinnamon buns and pancake breakfasts were a delight to wilderness adventurers and paddlers. Pilots often landed at his cabin beside the lake to take some of his baked goods home.

John managed to acquire ownership of the old family homestead on Lonesome Lake and was in the process of restoring it as a heritage site when it was destroyed by a forest fire in 2004. Undaunted, he constructed a small cabin at the old homesite with the help of friends and neighbours and continued to live there until his death in 2007.

After the death of her husband, Jack, Trudy left the Bella Coola Valley with her daughter Susan and son-in-law Tom Loosmore, and they relocated to Falkland in the North Okanagan, where the drier climate would be easier on Trudy's arthritis.

John Edwards after the devastating Lonesome Lake fire in 2004. Sage Birchwater photo

I happened to meet them on their exodus across the Chilcotin Plateau when we both stopped at the Tŝideldel gas bar on Redstone Flats. They were riding in two vehicles with various cats, dogs, chickens, horses and maybe a goat. It was an iconic moment, like running into the Beverly Hillbillies on Route 66, and I made a point of greeting Trudy and wishing her well.

Much has been written about this family of Lonesome Lake, beginning with Leland Stowe's *Crusoe of Lonesome Lake* (Random House, 1957), followed by Trudy Turner's *Fogswamp: Living with Swans in the Wilderness* (Hancock House, 1977), co-authored with Ruth

M. McVeigh; Ralph's posthumous memoir, *Ralph Edwards of Lonesome Lake*, as told to Ed Gould (Hancock House, 1979); Isabel Edwards's *Ruffles on My Longjohns* (Hancock House, 1980); and lastly Trudy's second book, *Packtrains & Airplanes: Memories of Lonesome Lake* (Hancock House, 2012).

JOHN EDWARDS AND VICKY THE FOX

My sons Junah and Shiney and I flew into Turner Lake in 1993 and rented a canoe from John Edwards to paddle the Turner Lake Chain to Cutthroat Lake, Vista Lake, Junker Lake and Widgeon Lake. Of course we had a feed of cinnamon buns and a pancake breakfast at John's bistro on the lake. John was a lively sixty-six years old at that time, with the vigour of a man half his age.

Three or four years later John and I connected again. We were both fire wardens for the Fire Protection Branch of the BC Forest Service. I monitored campsites across the Chilcotin Plateau from Kleena Kleene to Big Creek, and John called in the weather reports from Lonesome Lake on his hand-held Forest Service radio.

In July 2004 I was working as a staff reporter for the *Williams Lake Tribune* when the Lonesome Lake Fire destroyed John's dream to restore the old homestead begun by his father in 1913. He was seventy-seven years old.

John and thirteen firefighters were helicoptered to safety after their attempts to set up a sprinkler system to protect the homestead buildings were thwarted when the wind changed direction and the fire suddenly expanded. John was heartbroken because he figured the fire could have been extinguished a month earlier, when it was small, after it was started by a lightning strike on the ridge between Lonesome and Turner Lakes. It was left to burn because it was in Tweedsmuir Provincial Park and was a low priority to the Forest Service. (Government policy is to allow natural events like wildfires and epidemics like mountain pine beetle infestations to run their course in provincial parks without human intervention.)

The big thing for John was his pet fox, Vicky, whom he was feeding before being evacuated. Just before he was airlifted to safety he gave her one last meal. She was part of three generations of foxes he had befriended. He also had feeding stations for martens who visited him regularly. He said these were his family.

"Up until yesterday I could tell people I had a family. My little guys wore fur coats and they all had bushy tails," John told me. "Foxy lived with me for nine years, her daughter Vicky has now been with me two years, and she had her first puppies this spring."

The good news out of all this tragedy and heartbreak was that Vicky the fox emerged from the rubble unscathed as friends and volunteers helped John build a new home at the Birches. The young fox must have had an underground burrow that protected her from the inferno.

So John Edwards was given one last reprieve as he regrouped on his family's heritage property and spent his last years there in the company of his furry friends.

SUSAN TURNER'S LEGACY

When her mother, Trudy Turner, died in 2020, Susan Turner inherited the mantle as the eldest member of the Edwards family of Lonesome Lake.

Growing up in isolation with no other kids around and getting her formal education through the province's correspondence program had presented its own set of challenges. It was sometimes difficult for her to socialize with other children her own age.

"Growing up in the back of beyond as an only child, I didn't really know how to relate to other kids," she told me. "I was a very old child. It was easier for me to understand and speak to adults. My upbringing was much softer and more indulgent than my mom's. We had more conveniences and the farms were more established. Of course my mother had her two older brothers for company, whereas I had no siblings.

"The nice thing about taking correspondence, you had the freedom to change your schedule with the seasons. I took the summer off and did my schoolwork throughout the winter. Now a lot more people are doing home-schooling.

"I stopped formal schooling in grade eight and left home when I was pretty young. I was in and out a lot after I was sixteen, working at different jobs. Probably gone more than I was at home. Then I moved out on my own when I was twenty and went to Ontario for a while. Eventually I got my grade twelve with the GED after my kids were born."

Susan was only six years old when her grandfather Ralph Edwards flew off to Oona River and established his home there.

"I don't really have many memories of him at all, which is sad," she said. "I would have lots of questions for him if I could meet him now."

Like her mother and uncles before her, Susan got a significant amount of her learning from books.

"We had a decent number of books at home, but mostly we borrowed books from the Lending Library in Victoria. We'd go out for mail every six weeks and would come home with fifteen or twenty pounds of books we'd have to backpack home. Most of the books were hardcover in those days, so that made them heavier," she said.

"One of my favourite activities at Lonesome Lake was feeding the swans. It was pretty cool—the annual thing that we'd do every winter. For the first fifteen years of my life, until 1974, we horse-packed all the grain for the swans from the end of the road to Lonesome Lake. Leapfrogging, we'd horse-pack from Maxie Heckman's cabin at Atnarko to the bottom of Stillwater Lake, move it up the lake by raft, then horse-pack it to Lonesome Lake where we'd raft it up the lake to home. For me it was always the great adventure of the year. That six or seven weeks every fall I thought was the greatest thing in the world. It was something I looked forward to. Besides the fourteen thousand pounds of grain in hundred-pound sacks, there were grocery things. My dad always ordered a few luxury items we couldn't grow at Lonesome Lake, like cereal, Campbell's mushroom soup, bacon and Rogers Golden Syrup. Then there were the new books from the library. It was pretty exciting. We trekked back and forth, two trips a day with the horses. That's 140 sacks of grain. Thinking of my parents trying to keep track of me as a young kid, it must have been nerve-racking. I didn't think much of it. That's just what we did.

"We were always figuring out ways to achieve things. If you want something bad enough, you'll find a way to do it. Somebody asked my uncle John if he ever failed at anything. He answered, 'Yes, we failed many times. We just never gave up.'"

Susan said her two uncles had quite different personalities.

"John was a very precise person. Quite meticulous when he built things. Stanley was all about big ideas. John went to college in Alberta and learned filmmaking skills. Then he made films with his movie camera and took his lectures all over North America. He also babysat logging camps along the coast when they were closed down for the winter. That's how he made enough money to buy back the Birches from the California couple Ralph sold it to."

Today Susan lives in Falkland with her husband, Tom Loosmore, and their two sons, Brendon and Alex. Brendon and Alex each have their own place on the acreage they share, where they live with their kids Sasha, eleven, and Kayden, seven.

"We've got six horses," Susan said. "I got the horses for the grandkids, but they're not too interested. One of the horses is an offspring from Lonesome Lake. But he's a gelding, so he's the end of the line."

Susan noted that her grandfather's memoir, *Ralph Edwards of Lonesome Lake*, was finished by Ed Gould and published in 1979, two years after Ralph died.

"I never did see Ralph's original autobiography that Ed Gould used to write the book. I'd love to track it down and learn a bit more clearly who my grandfather actually was."

TOMMY WALKER

Tommy Walker was larger than life in the Atnarko country of the upper Bella Coola Valley. He left a big footprint in his nineteen years in the region. Decades after he left for the Spatsizi Plateau in northern British Columbia in 1948, people in the Bella Coola Valley and West Chilcotin still talked about him as if he had been there yesterday. He made that kind of an impact.

He was twenty-five when he came to the Bella Coola Valley from England in 1929 with his companion and benefactor, A.J. Arnold, a well-heeled member of the British upper class. As they stepped off the SS *Cardena* onto the docks in Bella Coola in September, stock markets around the world were poised to crash.

Walker grew up in England with a penchant for wilderness. This was largely inspired by the writings of Ernest Thompson Seton, a naturalist and Boy Scouts of America founder. Walker worked in the brewery business in London for four years, which took him to North America and California in particular in search of barley suitable for making the finest malt. That's how he gained a taste for the Pacific coast and a curiosity about British Columbia.

Back in London, Walker learned of the Bella Coola Valley from the agent general for British Columbia, F.A. Pauline, who agreed to rent him a log cabin he owned at Stuie along the Atnarko River for five dollars a month. This gave the two young adventurers a destination to begin their quest. In his 1976 memoir, *Spatsizi*, Walker describes the Bella Coola Valley and the people who populated the place at that moment in time.

He met B.F. (Bernard Fillip) Jacobsen, whose writings forty years earlier had inspired Norwegians from Minnesota to colonize the valley in 1894.

Gyllenspetz, a rough and ready Swedish-born bachelor, outfitter and trapper at Stuie, was still building the unfinished log cabin that Walker and Arnold had rented from Pauline in London.

Bill Bowron was the telegraph operator at Atnarko, about ten miles (fifteen kilometres) farther up the trail beyond Stuie. Bert Robson and Maxie Heckman also lived there. Ralph Edwards, the legendary Crusoe of

Lonesome Lake, was another eighteen miles (thirty kilometres) past them.

Other characters in that landscape were Domas Squinas, Chief of the Ulkatcho First Nation at Anahim Lake and Ulkatcho Village. Squinas and his large extended family had a summer fishing camp at Stuie right beside Walker and Arnold's rented cabin.

Pete McCormick, a legendary freighter, packer and backwoodsman, once drove eight-horse teams up the Cariboo Road pulling freight wagons from Ashcroft to Barkerville. He now resided at Clearwater Lake near Kleena Kleene and guided horse expeditions into the mountains.

Also at Kleena Kleene was George Turner, a legendary trapper and frontiersman, and his Tŝilhqot'in wife, Louisa One-Eye, a woman of some acclaim. Rumour had it that Turner was an escaped outlaw from the States, a member of the Dalton Gang who got away after the last great and fatal bank heist the group tried to pull off in Coffeyville, Kansas, in 1892. It's said he fled to Canada and slipped across the border at Blaine, Washington, in an Indigenous woman's dugout canoe and made his way to Bella Coola from there. He denied it, of course, and had other explanations for his nefarious past.[27]

These people were all from "up top" on the Chilcotin Plateau and visited the Bella Coola Valley on occasions when it suited them. Memories of these individuals were kept alive in conversations around kitchen tables and campfires for decades afterwards.

At first Tommy Walker figured he might be able to make a living as a fur farmer. This ambition quickly faded once he realized how far away Atnarko was from a reliable food source for the animals. A mink farmer had already pulled up stakes at Stuie and moved to the Lower Mainland, where waste meat from nearby slaughterhouses was readily available.

Walker described in his memoir how the shock waves of the Great Depression hardly made a ripple on the subsistence lifestyle of the Bella Coola Valley, where money had always been in short supply.

Gyllenspetz cabin at Stuie. Tommy Walker and A.J. Arnold rented it from the British Columbia agent general before they left London in 1929, only to find it half finished when they got there. Tommy Walker photo from page 97 in his memoir *Spatsizi* [Antonson Publishing 1976]

27   A more detailed account of George Turner and Louisa One-Eye was published in *Chilcotin Chronicles: Stories of Adventure and Intrigue from British Columbia's Central Interior* (Caitlin Press, 2017)

"I was confident I could fit in with frontier living," he wrote. "I was learning essential skills such as how to use a crosscut saw and a double-bitted axe, but coming up with a livelihood presented a real problem."[28]

Back in England every available acre of even marginal land was put to some use. By comparison the untrammelled wilderness of the upper Bella Coola Valley was endless. Arnold and Walker were in different social realms. Arnold was financially secure thanks to the endowment he received from his aristocratic family, so he had few worries about how to sustain himself. But Walker had to find a way to earn a living. Both men saw the potential of building accommodations to house visitors wanting to explore the pristine beauty of the region.

"We decided to build a lodge," Walker wrote. "All I could contribute was the labour."[29]

Fortunately A.J. Arnold had the resources to pay the bills to get the project off the ground, and he didn't seem to mind.

By the spring of 1930 they had the foundations for their new lodge well started when the first Dakelh and Tŝilhqot'in people rode down from the Chilcotin Plateau to go fishing in the Atnarko River. Walker observed the procession.

"The head of each family led a mounted entourage of women and children," he wrote. "Occasionally a very old lady walked behind, clutching a homemade staff."[30]

Gyllenspetz had told him about the Indigenous people from the high country who came down to the Atnarko Valley every spring to catch salmon before haying season.

"Watch for Chief Domas Squinas, head of the Ulkatcho People of Anahim Lake," he advised Walker. "He will camp at the smokehouse on top of the hill."

Walker had fenced off his property at the foot of the sandhill next to his cabin before Chief Squinas arrived. He was miffed when Squinas started packing water through his gate without asking permission. "This was contrary to English protocol and I expressed my displeasure to Chief Squinas," Walker confessed.

He said the Chief wasn't amused.

"Maybe I shoot you. I stop here a long time before you come," Squinas told Walker.

Walker realized he had bitten off more than he could chew taking on the Chief, and he quickly realized that he and Squinas had to make a truce.

"I was able to appreciate the Chief's view that I was the interloper," Walker acknowledged. "As a result we did not declare war and we soon became friends, bonded by a mutual respect."

---

28 Tommy Walker, *Spatsizi* (Surrey, BC: Antonson, 1976), 30–31.

29 Walker, *Spatsizi*, 31.

30 The following segment contains excerpts from Walker, *Spatsizi*, 32–33.

Domas Squinas, patriarch of the Squinas Family and Chief of the Ulkatcho Dakelh, had a ranch at Anahim Lake and a seasonal fishing camp right next to where Tommy Walker and A.J. Arnold built their lodge. Harlan I. Smith photo, Image 621437, courtesy Canadian Museum of History

Domas Squinas and his extended family at their summer camp in Stuie, next to Tommy Walker's lodge along the Atnarko River. Harlan I. Smith photo, Image 62182, courtesy Canadian Museum of History

A few years later Chief Squinas built a fence of his own around his nearby smokehouse.

"Squinas stop inside; policeman stop outside," he told Walker.

Apparently the local police and Indian agent authorities had been hassling Squinas for making homebrew, and this was his way to establish some boundaries.

In the summer of 1930, Pete McCormick and Austin Hallows, another frontiersman, from Anahim Lake, showed up with a string of horses to transport some mining prospectors up the Nuxalk-Dakelh Grease Trail into Thunder Mountain to do some drilling. Hallows encouraged Walker to learn how to pack horses as a way to earn some income.

"You should have a trade," he told Walker. "With a few head of horses you could make a little money."[31]

Little by little Walker was putting together the rudimentary tools to sustain himself in the bush. Gyllenspetz taught him how to pack, and when Bowron was offered a job running the telegraph office in Bella Coola, he sold him his pack horse Charlie for twenty-five dollars. Then Walker bought a saddle from Pete McCormick for another twenty-five dollars and was on his way. Austin Hallows taught him how to shoe his horse by driving a bevelled nail through the shoe and into the hoof so it

---

31 Walker, *Spatsizi*, 33.

Patrick Jack leads a horse over a bridge spanning turbulent Young Creek on the trail to the Chilcotin Plateau. Patrick Jack collection

emerged at just the right spot on the edge of the hoof to be broken off and clinched to hold the shoe tight.

Walker's first expedition was with Maxie Heckman, who needed to put a new roof on one of his trapping cabins. Heckman had been blown from a mining tunnel as a young man in Germany and had lost his left hand, but he had become quite adept at using his leather-covered stump together with his good hand to live a relatively active and functional life. Heckman Pass at the top of the Bella Coola Hill is named after him.

"Maxie gave me my first lesson in packing," Walker wrote in his memoir. "He said you have to keep the load balanced on either side of the saddle or you'll have to keep stopping to fix it."[32]

As the summer progressed, work on the lodge continued and Walker got more accustomed to the routines in the valley. Mail was driven up the valley twice a month from Hagensborg. Each week everything in the valley centred on "boat day" when the steamship arrived on Thursdays.

Before Bill Bowron moved to Bella Coola, he persuaded Walker to have a telephone installed in his log cabin. A single-strand telephone line had been stretched all the way from 150 Mile House to Bella Coola. In some places it was attached to trees.

Bowron brought a phone over to his cabin and screwed it to the log wall. A box beneath the mouthpiece housed two round batteries, and a

---

32   Walker, *Spatsizi*, 34.

Tommy Walker rows pack-horse supplies across the Atnarko River, helped by Colonel Cholmley in the water, in 1939. Cliff Kopas photo courtesy Leslie Kopas

long-handled receiver hung on a hook. Then Bowron installed a short metal horn just above the phone. Walker was curious.

"What on earth is that?" he asked.

"Oh that's a howler," Bowron replied. "When you want to make a call make sure the line is free and you don't have to lift the receiver. All the calls and conversations come through the howler."

Walker described it as a community gramophone.

"That's why all telegrams coming in and out of Bella Coola were quite public," he noted.[33]

The next spring Andy Holte, who had arrived in the Chilcotin from Washington State by covered wagon in 1922 and lived with his family at the Engebretson ranch at Towdystan, brought some horses down for Walker. "That must have been a hell of a good party you had last winter," he said.[34]

"How was that?" Walker replied. He was curious.

"Someone from your lodge was talking on the phone to Bowser at Anahim Lake and you were making such a racket the noise in our howler made the dogs bark."

Walker blushed. "That must have been when [Antone] Capoose came down with some fur to trade with Andy Christensen.

"We had a bit of a celebration, and Andy was dancing with old Antone beating time with a sooty frying pan on the old man's behind. I wonder what his old lady said when he got home and she had to clean the blackened buckskin?"

33   Walker, *Spatsizi*, 28.

34   The following segment contains excerpts from Walker, *Spatsizi*, 41–42.

"Wish I'd been there," Andy replied ruefully. "Not too many parties in our country. Peaches are too expensive." (Dried peaches made the best homebrew.)

Walker assured Holte there weren't many dried peaches in Atnarko either, then added he was rather proud of this accomplishment because not many parties could make dogs bark a hundred kilometres away.

Tommy Walker's cabin in Mackenzie Valley. Tommy Walker photo, page 102 in his memoir *Spatsizi* [Antonson Publishing 1976]

Tommy Walker and A.J. Arnold built their Stuie Lodge near the site of the ancient Nuxalk village of Stuic. The smallpox epidemic of 1862 had decimated the Nuxalk population and hastened the abandonment of this once great Nuxalk settlement, but it's no wonder the Nuxalk chose this as a village site. The climate near the confluence of the Atnarko and Talchako Rivers offers the best of both worlds for living conditions in the Bella Coola Valley. For one thing, it is far enough from the coast to be out of the relentless downpour of the rainforest. Yet the low elevation of the valley bottom forty miles (sixty-five kilometres) inland from tidewater provides a moderating coastal influence, keeping winter temperatures considerably warmer than on the high Chilcotin Plateau nearby. When it's −58°F (−50°C) at Anahim Lake, it might dip to only −14°F (−10°C) at Stuie.

Then there's the sunlight to consider. The Bella Coola Valley with its east-west orientation has many locations that don't see direct sunshine for months at a time during winter. The Talchako River flowing in a north-south direction creates a year-long window for winter sunshine.

The third aspect of Stuie's ideal winter climate has to be experienced to be fully understood. British Columbia has the phenomenon of frigid outflow winds blowing from the high interior of the province to the coast in wintertime. In the Bella Coola Valley the Nuxalk have a specific name for it: the *sps*. In translation it means "east wind." All coastal fjord valleys with outflow winds have one characteristic in common: the closer you get to tidewater, the greater the velocity of the outflow wind.

So say temperatures are −58°F (−50°C) in Anahim Lake and −14°C (−10°C) at Stuie, it might be only 23 or 25°F (−4 or −5°C) at the mouth of the Bella Coola River, but the *sps* is howling. In Anahim Lake at that moment there would likely not be any wind blowing at all.

At Stuie the outflow wind might be noticeable but minor, maybe only a couple of knots (four kilometres per hour). But in Bella Coola the *sps* could be ripping at twenty or thirty knots (forty or fifty-five kilometres per hour) and the wind chill would be extreme. The old Norwegians would spray water on the up-valley sides of their timber log houses to form a solid sheet of ice to keep the east wind from penetrating through the cracks.

So Stuie has ideal winter conditions. Slightly colder temperatures and snow that stays longer on the ground than at tidewater, but far less wind chill. And sunshine on those bitterly cold days is particularly welcome. All said, a great location for a village, and an ideal place to build a lodge.

Molly Walker and an unkown man in Bella Coola. Photo courtesy Clint Thompson

In May 1931, Walker's mother, Edith Etheldred Walker, and sister Molly arrived from England for a visit. Life in the Canadian wilds appealed to them, so they both decided to stay. Shortly after they settled in, Walker made his first foray into the high country of the Chilcotin Plateau with Andy Christensen, who asked him to do the census east of Stuie.

In June 1931, Walker set out on horseback with Andy and Dorothy Christensen to do the census. Dorothy wanted to check out some property her family owned at Anahim Lake. They liked what they saw, and soon after that, she and Andy put down roots in the upper country and established Cless Pocket Ranch. It became one of the more successful ranching operations in the area.

For several years while their children were growing up, Andy and Dorothy would spend the summers ranching in Anahim Lake and their winters in Bella Coola, where their kids could go to school. Andy ran the family store there, established three decades earlier by his father, Adolph Christensen.

Doing the census gave Walker his first real chance to look around the upper country and see where people lived. He met Frank Render at Lillie Lake, Andy Holte at Towdystan, George Powers at Charlotte Lake, Lester Dorsey and Austin Hallows at Three Circle Ranch, Chief Domas Squinas at Anahim Lake and George Turner and Pete McCormick at Kleena Kleene. He described the West Chilcotin as the last stand of the great Western ideology, where land could be staked and the frontiers of civilization pushed back.

Walker's mother and sister settled into Stuie Lodge, but soon Edith expressed a desire for a home of her own. Over the winter Walker went to work building one for her.

"Winter was a good time to log and start building," he stated in his memoir.[35]

With the help of a young Norwegian man recently arrived from Europe, he cleared a site next to the river with an unrestricted view of the mountains. Then, as each round of logs was notched and laid in place, his Norwegian craftsman flattened the insides of the logs with a broad axe. Soon the two-storey structure with an upstairs porch was complete. By spring, they were able to move in.

The following summer of 1932, Walker got his first look at the Rainbow Mountains when

Tommy Walker and his mother, Edith Etheldred Walker, in front of the house Tommy rebuilt for her after fire destroyed her first home in 1935. Photo courtesy Tommy Walker collection, page 98, *Spatsizi* [Antonson Publishing, 1976]

Nifty Merkel took him on a horseback venture. He was so impressed with the scenic beauty of the multicoloured lava peaks that he wrote a description of it for the *Times* of London. He doubted that his literary piece would ever be published, but to his surprise it was. Then he got a response from a wealthy manufacturer of health foods, Richard Maurice, who said he wanted to visit the country.

"He asked about a camping trip," Walker wrote. "We exchanged letters and he became my first trail-riding client."[36]

Something new was in the wind that would have a lasting impact on the whole country and Tommy Walker's future in particular. Around 1934 a civil servant in Victoria, John A.E. Collins, started spearheading a petition to have the government create a wilderness preserve from Ootsa Lake to the Bella Coola Valley.

Collins, a forest reconnaissance officer with the Department of Lands and Forests, was hired to do an inventory of the vast unsurveyed timbered areas of the province. He was concerned for the future of this scenic strip

---

35   Walker, *Spatsizi*, 42.

36   Walker, *Spatsizi*, 44.

of tableland beneath the eastern summits of the Coast Mountains. Its mosaic lakes and volcanic domes stretched 100 miles (160 kilometres) north from Walker's lodge at Stuie to the Nechako drainage of Ootsa Lake. Collins had the foresight that easy access into this natural treasure of wilderness would destroy it.

When Walker took his British client, Richard Maurice, on an excursion through the Rainbow Mountains, Collins asked him to take notes and photographs. Their 200-mile (320-kilometre) epic journey followed the Nuxalk-Dakelh Grease Trail over the Rainbow Mountains to the Dean River, then looped back up the Dean River to Anahim Lake and back to Stuie, following Chief Domas Squinas's route through the Precipice Valley.

That fall, the Walkers experienced a tragedy. On November 17, 1935, fire destroyed the house Walker had built for his mother. "We were left with the clothes we wore," he recounted, "without even a toothbrush to clean our teeth."[37] Undaunted, Walker started rebuilding in the spring, this time using a sawmill to fashion the logs into timbers. By fall of 1936, they were able to move in. More than eighty years later, this beautiful building still stands.

That same fall, while Walker was guiding duck hunters in Anahim Lake, A.J. Arnold returned to England on urgent family business. A few months later Walker received a letter from Arnold saying he couldn't return. For the Walkers, this presented a problem because Arnold's independent wealth had financed the operation of the lodge and made the payments on the land.

As luck would have it, Walker's fortunes took a turn for the better. Thanks to the lobbying of John A.E. Collins, the provincial government announced plans to reserve a great wilderness area between the Bella Coola Valley and Ootsa Lake embracing over 5,000 square miles (13,000 square kilometres). Walker said later he heard the reserve would be a provincial park named after the newly appointed Governor General of Canada, John Buchan, first Baron Tweedsmuir.[38] On top of that, the Governor General and his wife, Susan Buchan, were going to visit the following summer to inspect this territory. Part of the celebration was slated for Tommy Walker's Stuie Lodge.

A royal visit from the King's official representative in Canada created quite a stir. The Governor General indicated he and his wife would enjoy a camping trip. Up until that time, the only trails through the Rainbow Mountains were those used by the Dakelh and Tŝilhqot'in inhabitants descending the precarious switchbacks from the high plateau country into the Bella Coola Valley.

---

37 Walker, *Spatsizi*, 47.
38 Walker, *Spatsizi*, 49.

Stuie Lodge, built by Tommy Walker and A.J. Arnold in 1930, was later renamed Tweedsmuir Lodge with Lord Tweedsmuir's blessing. Photo Tommy Walker collection, page 100, *Spatsizi* [Antonson Publishing 1976].

At first it was proposed that Lord and Lady Tweedsmuir would travel on horseback from Ootsa Lake to the Bella Coola Valley. Then it was downsized to flying the regal party into Tanyez Tezdli and proceeding from there on horseback to Stuie Lodge in the Atnarko Valley. That's how it sat when several Ulkatcho families who lived in the region were hired to build more than twenty miles (thirty-two kilometres) of new trails through the Rainbow Mountains. Bridges were constructed over creeks, corduroy was laid through swampy sections, and switchbacks were dug into the steep slopes. Andy Cahoose and Henry Jack, who were Ulkatcho Elders when I met them in the 1990s, were youngsters when they helped their parents, George and Mary Cahoose and Jamos and Emma Jack, transform their old trails into a backwoods highway. It meant employment for Tommy Walker too.

"At least I had steady work for my pack outfit, carrying supplies to the road-building crew every week."[39]

In the end, the trail-building efforts for the Governor General were all for naught. The cross-country horseback venture was cancelled when a cavalcade of provincial politicians wanted to join the expedition. Lord Tweedsmuir's wish for a simple camp-out with his wife in the Rainbow Mountains never materialized.

---

39   Walker, *Spatsizi*, 51.

After an official reception on the shores of Ootsa Lake in the northern part of the new park, Lord and Lady Tweedsmuir were flown directly to Bella Coola and driven up the valley to Tommy Walker's lodge at Stuie.

"There, enraptured by the wild mountain scenery, they enjoyed an intimate meeting with settlers of that remote region," Walker wrote. "The Governor General's standard waved from our flagstaff for five days."[40]

Walker said anticipation for the extravagant safari brought him a much-needed influx of cash and a well-graded trail into the Rainbow Mountains. Lord Tweedsmuir also granted permission to change the name of his lodge from Stuie Lodge to Tweedsmuir Lodge.

JOHN BUCHAN: FIRST BARON TWEEDSMUIR

Canada's fifteenth Governor General, the first Baron Tweedsmuir of Elsfield, came from humble beginnings. John Buchan was a commoner born in Perth, Scotland, on August 26, 1875. He grew up in Kirkcaldy, Fife, where his father was a minister for the Free Church of Scotland.

His summer holidays spent in the Scottish Borders country helped instill an appreciation for nature, a love for walking and a fondness for local scenery and wildlife. At an early age Buchan showed an aptitude for writing. At seventeen he received a scholarship to the University of Glasgow, where he studied classics, wrote poetry and became a published author.

At twenty he received a scholarship to Brasenose College, Oxford. By the time he graduated he had authored and edited five books. Throughout his prolific literary career he published over 100 books, including 29 novels, 42 non-fiction accounts, 10 biographies, 4 books of poetry and 14 edited works.

Buchan graduated from Oxford with a law degree in 1901 and entered the diplomatic service as the private secretary to Alfred Milner, High Commissioner for South Africa and other colonies. Here his experiences provided the background for a series of adventure novels that brought him widespread acclaim. His most famous spy-thriller novel, *The Thirty-Nine Steps*, was later made into a motion picture by Alfred Hitchcock.

When Buchan returned to London after a couple of years in South Africa, he resumed his writing career as editor of the *Spectator*, a prestigious political magazine. He married Susan Charlotte Grosvenor in 1907, and the couple had four children together.

With the outbreak of the First World War, Buchan used his literary skills to write for the British War Propaganda Bureau as a correspondent in France.

---

40 Walker, *Spatsizi*, 51.

Buchan visited Canada for the first time in 1924 as a guest of Prime Minister William Lyon Mackenzie King. The prime minister was impressed by Buchan's knowledge of Canada and his writing about the Canadian Forces fighting in Europe during the First World War as a journalist with the *Spectator*. King recommended Buchan as a suitable successor to Governor General Lord Byng of Vimy, but Buchan declined the appointment because Canada and Great Britain were tangled in a constitutional dispute. The dispute arose because Governor General Byng refused to dissolve parliament as King requested, and this refusal was seen as interference by the British government in Canada's affairs. The dispute was resolved in 1931 with the passage of the Statute of Westminster, and this proved to be pivotal in the relationship between Great Britain and its former colonies. Essentially it ensured that the British government could no longer legislate for its independent Commonwealth countries. Thus Canada's sovereignty was enshrined.

John and Susan Buchan (Lord and Lady Tweedsmuir). John Buchan was Canada's fifteenth Governor General from 1935–1940. Image G-03506 courtesy of the Royal BC Museum and Archives

Buchan entered politics when he was elected to the British House of Commons in 1927 as the Unionist Party member for the Combined Scottish Universities. He was a popular politician but lacked the drive and partisan fervour for a cabinet post.

In Canada Mackenzie King's Liberals were defeated in 1930 by R.B. (Richard Bedford) Bennett's Conservatives. Mired in the Great Depression, people couldn't afford gas for their cars, so they took out the engines and windows and transformed the chassis into horse-drawn wagons. These vehicles were called "Bennett buggies" after the prime minister. In the United States they were called "Hoover carts" after President Herbert Hoover.

In 1935 Prime Minister Bennett resubmitted John Buchan's name for Governor General. This time Buchan accepted. On March 27, 1935, the Canadian Parliament announced that King George V had approved John Buchan as Canada's fifteenth Governor General. It took nearly eight months for Buchan to be officially sworn in, and by that time many changes had taken place, including a transformation of Buchan's identity.

Buchan was a commoner when King George V approved his appointment as Canada's next Governor General, but the monarch wanted a nobleman as his viceregal representative. Mackenzie King, then leader of the Opposition, figured a commoner holding the King's gavel was a good thing. The debacle that had led to the Statute of Westminster was still fresh in his mind. But King George V would not be swayed. On June 1, 1935, he elevated Buchan to the peerage, entitling him as the first Baron Tweedsmuir of Elsfield in the county of Oxford.

By the time Lord Tweedsmuir was officially sworn into office on November 2, 1935, Mackenzie King was prime minister again after defeating Bennett in an October election. The tides of change continued to envelop the new Governor General when the British monarch passed away on January 20, 1936.

King George V was succeeded by his eldest son, King Edward VIII. However, 326 days later he abdicated, giving way to his younger brother, King George VI, who was crowned on December 11, 1936.

That's how Buchan began his five-year appointment as Governor General, representing three monarchs in just over a year's time. He also travelled widely throughout the country, striving to unify the diverse cultural components that make up Canada. In 1937 he became the first Governor General to visit the Arctic, and it was on this journey that he visited Tweedsmuir Provincial Park, named in his honour, in British Columbia.

On August 15, 1937, Lord and Lady Tweedsmuir got off the train in Burns Lake and travelled by motor car to Ootsa Lake. A great encampment had been set up to accommodate them while they explored the scenic wonders in the northern areas of the park by boat and float plane.

After several days they flew to Bella Coola to visit the southern entrance to the park. That's where they met Tommy Walker, his mother, Edith, and his sister Molly at Stuie Lodge.

"We set up a large camp in a clearing across the road from the lodge," Walker wrote in his memoir. "A line of large banquet tents with silverware to grace the tables faced a row of smaller tents for the waiters, flunkies, cooks and other help."[41]

Once the retinue of provincial politicians had returned by gunboat to Victoria, Lord and Lady Tweedsmuir enjoyed a quiet respite at Stuie Lodge, visiting with Edith Walker and other residents living in the remote wilds of the region. Walker noted that John Buchan, the author of so many adventure books before he became Lord Tweedsmuir, walked through the forest of Atnarko with his alpenstock (an

---

41   Walker, *Spatsizi*, 51.

iron-tipped hiking pole) and listened to his sister Molly's adventure stories about grizzly bears.

The following spring, a large crate of plants arrived in Stuie from Rideau Hall in Ottawa.

"Lady Tweedsmuir sent them to my mother as she had been impressed with her determination to have a flower garden around our log house," Walker wrote.[42]

In 1938 Tweedsmuir Provincial Park was officially proclaimed in the Governor General's honour, and with the Governor General's permission, Stuie Lodge adopted a new name, Tweedsmuir Lodge.

In the foreword to a booklet published to commemorate his visit, Lord Tweedsmuir wrote, "I have now travelled over most of Canada and have seen many wonderful things, but I have seen nothing more beautiful and more wonderful than the great park which British Columbia has done me the honour to call by my name."[43]

John Buchan, Lord Tweedsmuir, died in office while still serving as Governor General. He collapsed from a stroke while shaving and suffered a severe head injury when he fell. He passed away on February 11, 1940.

In his nearly five years as Governor General, Lord Tweedsmuir contributed much to the Canadian cultural mosaic. He and Lady Tweedsmuir established the first proper library at Rideau Hall in Ottawa.

As a prolific author, he founded the prestigious Governor General's Literary Awards in 1936. This was done in conjunction with the Canadian Authors Association, recognizing the best writers in Canada.

Buchan encouraged a distinct Canadian identity and national unity and raised the ire of some imperialists when he said that a Canadian's first loyalty was to Canada and Canada's king, not to the British Commonwealth of Nations.

He also encouraged ethnic groups to maintain their individuality and each make their contributions to the national character of the country.

"The strongest nations are those that are made up of different racial elements," he stated.[44]

---

42   Walker, *Spatsizi*, 52.

43   John Buchan, quoted in "Tweedsmuir South Provincial Park," BC Parks, https://bcparks.ca/explore/parkpgs/tweeds_s/nat_cul.html#History.

44   John Buchan, quoted in Doug Saunders, "Canada's Mistaken Identity," *Globe and Mail*, June 26, 2009, https://www.theglobeandmail.com/news/world/canadas-mistaken-identity/article787370/.

THE TREK TO SPATSIZI

Patrick Jack and Albert Casimer were both young men when Tommy Walker hired them to help take his string of pack horses and saddle horses 900 miles (1,450 kilometres) from the Bella Coola Valley to the Spatsizi Plateau. The year was 1948, and it was an epic journey. More than four decades later, Albert and Patrick, whom I befriended in Anahim Lake, still spoke of this adventure as if it had happened yesterday.

When Walker came to the Bella Coola Valley from England in 1929 and established tourist accommodations at Stuie, forty miles (sixty-five kilometres) up the valley from tidewater, it was still a pretty wild place. But after nineteen years there, the valley was becoming too civilized for his liking. By the late 1940s there were serious rumblings by valley residents to punch a road through the Coast Mountains past his lodge to link with the provincial highway grid. That would change the whole tone of the wilderness he craved so passionately.

Walker had advocated strongly for Tweedsmuir Provincial Park, which had been established ten years earlier in 1938. He reasoned that the wilderness preserve was a good way to safeguard the Indigenous way of life enjoyed by the Ulkatcho People for whom he had developed a great fondness. The *Ulkatchot'en* (people of the Ulkatcho First Nation) used the Rainbow Mountains and rich fur-bearing country along the Dean River north

Albert Casimer and Patrick Jack pack a horse on their epic trek with Tommy Walker from the Atnarko Valley to the Spatsizi Plateau in 1948. Patrick Jack collection

of Anahim Lake, and Walker could appreciate how the remoteness of the Ulkatcho homeland, equidistant from "inept government agencies," was their strongest asset to retaining their sovereignty and independence.[45]

"They were almost beyond reach of an indifferent officialdom of two Indian Agencies," Walker wrote in his memoir. "The park will protect the undisturbed ecology of the Ulkatcho homeland from unfettered development and the pressure of cattlemen seeking virgin pastures."

Walker said the settlers and Indigenous inhabitants were able to mingle easily in the freedom of an unrestrictive society, despite cultural differences.

"We didn't always understand each other's customs but neither did we meddle in the other's affairs," he wrote.

One of the great social successes was the annual stampede that Walker initiated on the flat next to his lodge at Stuie in 1933.

"Indians and settlers came from ranches and homesteads, from Ulkatcho to the Chilcotin," he wrote. "Chief Domas Squinas particularly enjoyed the gatherings because he was fond of a little gambling."

The bone game lahal, like other Indigenous practices such as the potlatch, had been outlawed by the federal government and was frowned on by police authorities and Indian agents, but this didn't deter Chief Squinas.

"Each night he'd sit on a block of wood in his smokehouse under the tall firs, and beat his drum in time with the lahal chant. Like a croupier, he'd watch the chanting teams," Walker wrote.

Patrick Jack remained inspired by his horse trek experience with Tommy Walker for his whole life. Sage Birchwater photo

Albert Casimer was nineteen when he helped Tommy Walker move his horses to the Spatsizi in 1948. Sage Birchwater photo

---

45 The following segment contains excerpts from Walker, *Spatsizi*, 52–53.

Everyone, Indigenous and settler, rode in the horse races and buck-ing contests. Walker noted, "It was easy for the settler and the aboriginal to merge with little friction in a wide land where there was scope for all."

As the pang of the Great Depression ended, Walker continued taking guests into the mountains on horseback. One group of clients consisted of twelve women and a man, and Walker didn't have difficulty persuad-ing his friend George Draney to guide them on the trail while he man-aged the lodge.

One of the riders, Marion Bullock-Webster, returned the following year, and while helping Walker take his horses to Anahim Lake for the win-ter, the two became engaged. They were married the following March.

Walker described in his memoir how wealthy VIPs from across the world sought out fishing and hunting opportunities in the raw Cana-dian wilderness to clear their minds of the stresses of their jobs. These were the clients he brought into the high country of Tweedsmuir park and the Chilcotin Plateau.

During the off-season, Tommy and Marion would travel around to visit their clients in Portland, Ore-gon, San Francisco, and oth-er metropolitan centres to drum up more business.

"I soon discovered that busy executives always found time to talk about hunt-ing and fishing," he wrote. "These men realized the need to recharge their bat-teries in the untamed sur-roundings close to nature."[46]

Not all VIPs were the same. Walker described a party of wealthy Americans from Chicago who arrived at the dock in Bella Coola with an arsenal of high-powered rifles stuffed into expensive

Marion and Tommy Walker at Cold Fish Lake on the Spatsizi Plateau in 1951. Tommy Walker collection, page 112, *Spatsizi* [Antonson Pub-lishing, 1976]

---

46   Walker, *Spatsizi*, 54.

scabbards. He said they looked grim in their new stetson hats with leather straps under their chins.

"It was my first experience with VIP hunters, and when I met them at the wharf, I was appalled."[47]

He compared this with Canadian industrialist H.R. MacMillan, who was also a client.

"When H.R. MacMillan arrived, he handed me his old weather-beaten Winchester .30.06 to put into the truck while he walked across the dock to shake hands with a local logger. He never forgot anyone who worked for him in the woods in the early days."[48]

It was through H.R. MacMillan that Walker got wind of the Spatsizi Plateau in northern British Columbia. After that, there was no turning back. In 1946, he and Marion sold Tweedsmuir Lodge to Colonel Gordon Corbould. By that time the citizens of the Bella Coola Valley, led by Cliff Kopas and Elijah Gurr, were stepping up their efforts for a road through the Coast Mountains to the Chilcotin Plateau. This assured the lodge a rosy future, but for the Walkers it spelled the end of their untrammelled wilderness.

Free of the fishing resort, they figured they would continue their horse-packing ventures without the added responsibilities of managing a lodge. Then the lure of the Spatsizi wilderness beckoned them. Over the winter of 1947–48, they prepared for their grand exodus—900 miles (1,450 kilometres) from the Bella Coola Valley to the Spatsizi Plateau.

What they hadn't anticipated was the record snowpack that occurred that winter across British Columbia. The spring freshets of 1948 burst the banks of the lower Fraser River, causing widespread flooding from Hope to Richmond. Bella Coola was similarly inundated with washouts and flooding as Tommy and Marion, along with their three wranglers, Patrick Jack, Albert Casimer and Colonel Mike TenBroeke, began their epic undertaking.

On May 26 they brought fifteen horses east from Stuie to Young Creek to find that one of the three stringers supporting the Young Creek bridge had washed out. Gingerly, they led one horse after another over the raging waters.

Ascending the steep precipice trail, they found more bridge washouts and high water. At Cless Pocket Ranch, Patrick and Albert said farewell to family and friends they wouldn't see until the fall. Their route would take them over the Itcha mountains into the Blackwater country to the Home Ranch of Pan Phillips, the pioneer American who came to the country with his sidekick Rich Hobson in 1934, searching for grass beyond the mountain.

---

47   Walker, *Spatsizi*, 60.
48   Walker, *Spatsizi*, 60–61.

The heavy snowfall had hit Pan hard too. He had run out of hay that winter and lost fifty head of horses, but he still had three horses to sell to Tommy. Patrick and Albert halter-broke the animals in an afternoon. They crossed the Blackwater River on a raft and swam the horses to the other side. Ten miles (sixteen kilometres) up the trail, Pan's horses bolted and returned home. The trekkers had no choice but to continue up the rough wagon road without them.

Tommy was able to procure more horses at Vanderhoof, and the party ran smack dab into the great racial prejudice of those times when Patrick and Albert were refused service in the Vanderhoof restaurant because they were Indigenous. However, Tommy and Marion met up with Rich Hobson and his wife, Gloria, who were friends with the hotel owner, and an exception was made to serve them as long as Patrick and Albert were with the Walkers. Such a sad statement of those times.

After resting up for a few days, Albert and Patrick drove the horses to Fort St. James, where Tommy arranged to have the horses and supplies barged up Stuart Lake and through rivers and waterways to the north end of Takla Lake. They had travelled 300 miles (480 kilometres) in twenty-five days to Fort St. James, one week behind schedule.

On June 28 they departed with the scows, crossing the threshold into the northern wilderness. Travelling with three scows lashed together was an ordeal. On July 1 they unloaded the horses at Takla Lake and continued their perilous journey overland, following the Driftwood River. They were now in country not settled by homesteaders, and each curve of the trail brought new adventures.

Finding sufficient feed for the animals remained a constant concern. Tommy reflected in his journal that Patrick, Albert and Mike all had a home to return to, but he and Marion were chasing a dream into an uncertain future.

"Our outfit—horses, saddles, tents and other equipment—was our livelihood, and we were carrying it all with us into a wilderness in quest of a dream valley."[49]

Albert returned home to Anahim Lake two weeks earlier than Patrick to make sure his grandmother Christine Squinas got her hay up. For both men, the journey to this faraway land broadened their horizons and changed their lives forever.

Tommy and Marion spent the next twenty-five years in the country known as British Columbia's Serengeti before retiring in Smithers in the mid-1970s.

---

49 Walker, *Spatsizi*, 118.

THE NUXALK-DAKELH GREASE TRAIL

There's probably not a more celebrated fish in the cultural history of British Columbia than the eulachon (also spelled oolichan). The fish itself is small in size, approximately twenty centimetres long and skinny like a sardine. But it packs a wallop. It is so full of nutrients, particularly fat, that once it has been dried it can be lit on fire like a candle, hence its other common name, candlefish.

The Nuxalk People of Bella Coola looked forward to the arrival of the *sputc* (their name for the eulachon) every spring in late March as their first feed of fresh fish for the year. They would enjoy this delicacy eaten fresh or smoked and dried. But the fish's rich fat content limited the number of fish most people could eat at a sitting. It wasn't the consumption of *sputc* for its flesh that caused the biggest stir, however. It was the rich polyunsaturated oil that could be extracted from them. Best known as eulachon grease, it was so highly prized as a trade commodity that the trails used to transport it inland from the coast were known as grease trails.

Numerous grease trails extended from the coast into the interior of the continent along North America's northwest coast from Oregon to Alaska, but few were better known than the Nuxalk-Dakelh (Carrier) Grease Trail—now also known as the Alexander Mackenzie Heritage Trail—which stretched 347 kilometres from Burnt Bridge in the Bella Coola Valley to the Fraser River near Quesnel. The Nuxalk and Dakelh Peoples used this trade route for thousands of years.

Signs marking the Nuxalk-Dakelh Grease Trail. Krystie Jimmie photo

Eulachon grease produced by the Nuxalk was traded to the Da-kelh and Tŝilhqot'in for soapberries, obsidian, tanned buckskin and dried meat. Grease was also traded to the Heiltsuk on the outer coast.

Family ties and intermarriage between the coastal and the interi-or peoples was a natural consequence of this trade and communication along the Nuxalk-Dakelh Grease Trail. Goodwill and understanding pre-vailed despite differences in culture, language and traditions.

With his foot resting on a dugout spoon canoe, Pat Schooner celebrates a successful harvest of eulachons in 1935. Cliff Kopas photo courtesy Leslie Kopas

ALEXANDER MACKENZIE

Mention of Alexander Mackenzie in association with the Nuxalk-Dakelh Grease Trail is still a sore point for many Southern Dakelh people, who feel that renaming it the Alexander Mackenzie Heritage Trail appropriates the significance of their ancient grease trail.

In 1793 the Scottish explorer working for the North West Company followed the Nuxalk-Dakelh Grease Trail from the Fraser River to the Pacific Ocean, thus becoming the first European recognized to have crossed North America by land north of Mexico. Mackenzie took this route on the advice of Dakelh people he met fishing in the Fraser River near the present-day city of Quesnel, and he hired Dakelh guides to show him the way.

Mackenzie left Montreal in 1792 on a quest to find a route to the Pacific Ocean for the fur trade. He got to the Fraser River in June the following year. Dakelh people he met there convinced him the quickest and easiest access to salt water was to abandon the southward-flowing Fraser River and follow the grease trail westward along the Blackwater River. Mackenzie named this tributary flowing into the Fraser the West Road River. At its headwaters they reached Ulkatcho Village, where Mackenzie described the Culla Culla potlatch house in his journal.[50]

Farther west at Tanya Lakes, originally named Tanyez Tezdli by the Dakelh people, they crossed the Rainbow Mountains to the Bella Coola Valley, where Mackenzie's party was welcomed by the Nuxalk in a village at the mouth of Burnt Bridge Creek. From there Nuxalk guides took him by canoe to the village of Q'umk'uts at the mouth of the Bella Coola River, where the explorer borrowed a canoe. They paddled several kilometres down the fjord to the Dean Channel, where Mackenzie made his famous inscription on a rock with vermilion and grease: "Alex Mackenzie from Canada by land 22nd July 1793."

Then Mackenzie's party departed the way they came, up the Bella Coola River to Burnt Bridge Creek and along the grease trail to the Fraser River, where they had left their canoes and a cache of supplies. They continued east and back to Montreal, and the Dakelh never saw Mackenzie again.

It wasn't until the mid-1970s that the shadow of Mackenzie's historic undertaking started to cloud Southern Dakelh sovereignty. Hälle Flygare, a Swedish-born Canadian working for Bob Stewart of Stewart's Lodge at Nimpo Lake, first got the idea to preserve the route Mackenzie had followed when he saw how industrial logging was threatening to obliterate eastern sections of the Nuxalk-Dakelh Grease Trail. He knew he had to act fast.

---

50   *Sir Alexander Mackenzie Heritage Trail (Retracing the Nuxalk-Carrier Grease Trail): A Photojournal by Hälle Flygare 1966–1986* (Nature in Wild Places, 2021), 57.

Non-Indigenous settlers and frontiersmen like Bob Stewart, Pan Phillips and Lester Dorsey, who guided hunters and fishers in the area, knew all about the grease trail. Dakelh families who lived along the trail still used it. But some sections of the original route were falling in, and new paths were chosen.

In 1975 Flygare and fellow conservancy advocate John Woodworth managed to persuade Parks Canada and BC Parks to fund an inventory of the route Mackenzie had followed, and big changes were in the wind. An overlay of Mackenzie's journey was placed on top of maps of the historic grease trail system, and work got underway to chart the route Mackenzie had followed.

Linda Flygare, Hälle's wife, described the work in their 2021 trail book *Nuxalk-Carrier Grease Trail*. "By the end of the following summer [of 1976], Halle and I had completed an inventory of the Trail between the Fraser River to Bella Coola Highway," she wrote. "We were assisted by two First Nations [Dakelh] Carriers, Wally Patrick and Stan Boyd. We documented ground cover, camping areas, drinking water sources, private land, Native reserves, trail conditions, and areas where the trail deviated from the original footpath to accommodate horses and wagons used after the 1920s."[51]

Then the Alexander Mackenzie Heritage Trail project took on a life of its own. Over the next twelve years, the Flygares and Woodworth started clearing and straightening the 347-kilometre overland route Mackenzie had followed between the Fraser River and the Bella Coola Valley. When they got to Tanyez Tezdli, 290 kilometres west of the Fraser River, the evidence of the grease trail over the Rainbow Mountains was still very much defined.

Linda Flygare wrote that Mackenzie's final route to the Pacific Ocean was decided for him once he reached Tanyez Tezdli. She quoted from Mackenzie's journal:

"I was now informed that some people of another tribe [Nuxalk] were sent for, who wished very much to see us. Two of them would accompany us over the mountains. This they undertook without the least hesitation; and, at the same time, pointed out to me the pass in the mountains, bearing south by east by compass."[52]

Flygare also mentions improvements to the trail in 1937, such as corduroy built over swampy sections by Ulkatcho families to accommodate John Buchan, first Baron Tweedsmuir and Canada's fifteenth Governor General, after whom Tweedsmuir Provincial Park was named. To celebrate

51   Linda Flygare, in *Nuxalk-Carrier Grease Trail: An Illustrated History from 1793 to 1986 of the First Nation Grease Trail Followed by Alexander Mackenzie […]*, vol. 1 of 3 (Nature in Wild Places, 2021), 2.

52   Flygare, in *Nuxalk-Carrier Grease Trail*, 3.

A pack string of horses traverses the open alpine along the Nuxalk-Dakelh Grease Trail through the Rainbow Mountains. Sage Birchwater photo

the creation of the park, the Governor General's party was scheduled to ride from Tanyez Tezdli to Stuie in the Bella Coola Valley, but plans changed and that never happened. Improvements to the trail made forty years earlier were still evident, however, when the Flygares mapped the route.

Mackenzie's crossing of North America took place a full twelve years before Americans Meriwether Lewis and William Clark performed a similar feat for the United States from the Mississippi River to the mouth of the Columbia River in 1805. As the identification of Mackenzie's route gained national significance, it overshadowed the origin, purpose and importance of the Nuxalk-Dakelh Grease Trail. It was a slow erosion of rights and recognition, typical of the colonial process in which Indigenous ownership of the land is minimized or lost.

In 1987 Stan Boyd, the elected Chief of the Nazko First Nation, had a front-row seat witnessing the hoopla over Mackenzie and the diminishing recognition of Dakelh ownership and control of the ancient grease trail used for millennia by his people.

"Mackenzie was the first European visitor to come to our country," Stan said in the 1987 documentary *Tanyez Tezdli*, produced by Quesnel School District 28. "He only walked down the trail once, yet the trail is named after him."[53]

---

53 *Tanyez Tezdli* (Quesnel, BC: School District 28, 1987), DVD.

A pack train follows single file along a narrow section of the Nuxalk-Dakelh Grease Trail in the Rainbow Mountains. Sage Birchwater photo

Stan watched as Hälle Flygare and John Woodworth surveyed and mapped the route followed by the Scottish explorer, identifying each camping place used by his party. In the process they used Mackenzie's diary and a distance-calculating wheel to publish a detailed trail guide, *In the Steps of Alexander Mackenzie*, in 1987.

In 1982 an agreement had been struck between the provincial and federal governments to officially designate Mackenzie's route from the Fraser River to the Pacific as the Alexander Mackenzie Grease Trail.

Then in 1983 the Master Development Plan dropped "Grease" from the official name because some members of the trail committee considered it offensive. So the trail got rebranded as the Alexander Mackenzie Heritage Trail, with "Nuxalk-Carrier Route" tagged on below in smaller print.

"It was the Dakelh people living alongside the trail who kept it open," Stan Boyd continued in the documentary. "It was our trail and we used it to get from one settlement to another. We should have had decision-making input into naming and managing this trail."

Ulkatcho Chief Jimmy Stillas also spoke in the documentary, describing his nation's use of the trail: "We used the grease trail from Bella Coola to Nazko, about five miles on either side. When we got to Bella Coola we traded dried meat and soapberries for eulachon grease. In Tanyez Tezdli we'd get together with the people of Nazko, Lhoosk'uz, Ootsa Lake and Bella Coola. It was a time to be together to communicate and renew our friendships with each other. We'd catch and dry fish and play a few games. Mostly we played lahal, though sometimes we had foot races, horse races or spear-throwing contests. Sometimes we had to walk back home from Tanyez Tezdli after losing our horses in a gambling game to some Nazko people."

Jimmy Stillas's mother, Mary Jane Stillas (McEwan), was the oldest child of Emma Stillas (Jack), the daughter of Baptiste and Betsie Stillas. Though Baptiste was Dakelh in language and tradition, he could trace his roots to one of five brothers who moved to the high country from the Nuxalk village of Stuic in the Bella Coola Valley.

Mary Jane's biological father, Joe Saunders, was Nuxalk from Kimsquit. Joe's oldest daughter, Margaret Siwallace, was Mary Jane's half-sister. So Jimmy Stillas and Margaret Siwallace's son Andy Siwallace were first cousins.

After Mary Jane was born, Emma married Jamos Jack, a Dakelh man from Cheslatta.

Ulkatcho Chief Jimmy Stillas lashes a sharpened fishing hook to a spear pole during the 1987 Ulkatcho gathering at Tanyez Tezdli. Sage Birchwater photo

Jimmy Stillas's biological father, David Moody, was Nuxalk from Bella Coola. After Jimmy was born, Mary Jane married Mack McEwan and they had a large family together.

This explains Jimmy Stillas's web of family ties to both the Nuxalk and Dakelh First Nations. In the *Tanyez Tezdli* documentary, he explained how these different cultural traditions played out on the land:

"We had five different trails leading into Bella Coola. The first couple went down the Atnarko River. The word *Atnarko* comes from two Dakelh words: *Atna*, meaning 'Bella Coola People,' and *Koh*, meaning 'valley.' Once you hit the big timber, you respected the Bella Coola People. When you were in the Jack pine country up top, you respected the Ulkatcho, Lhoosk'uz and Nazko People."

After Mary Jane married Mack McEwan, Jimmy was raised by his great-grandfather Baptiste Stillas along the grease trail between Ulkatcho Village and Tanyez Tezdli. In a personal interview I had with Jimmy shortly before his death in November 1990, he described their mobile way of life travelling about the country:

"When we're going to move from one camp to the next one, my grandfather decides that. He decides when we leave. 'Tomorrow we're going to Bella Coola,' he'd say. As soon as money came in, we had to trap beavers night and day to pay for the gun. My grandfather used poison parsnip to hunt beaver. He knew how to use it. Everybody had their specialty. Some people were fishers and others were hunters. Kids were ordered by the Elders to work. Grandpa Stillas was still the boss."

Mary Jane McEwan's younger brother Henry Jack was seven years old when Jimmy was born. Henry and Jimmy grew up together, and Henry shared many stories of their life along the grease trail and in the Ulkatcho heartland in the book *Ulkatcho Stories of the Grease Trail*.

THE ULKATCHO BOOK SERIES

In 1990, Chief Jimmy Stillas initiated a project to document Ulkatcho culture and history for the generations not yet born. His vision was to publish a series of books containing the words and stories of the Elders, complemented by archival photographs collected from a number of sources. I was hired as the writer and researcher, and Leona Toney and Janie Jack were the culture curriculum committee leaders directing the project. Numerous Ulkatcho Elders shared their knowledge, as did Elders from the Nuxalk community.

Sadly, Jimmy Stillas died in a snowmobiling accident before the first book, *'Ulkatchot'en: The People of Ulkatcho*, was published in 1991. Work on the project continued, however. The community was eager to publish a second book on the Nuxalk-Dakelh Grease Trail in time for the bicentennial of Alexander Mackenzie's historic 1793 journey.

The Elders wanted to set the record straight that the ownership of the trail still belonged to the Southern Dakelh Nation, and in 1993 *Ulkatcho Stories of the Grease Trail* was published. A third book, *Ulkatcho Food and Medicine Plants*, followed in 1996.

The Ulkatcho First Nation holds the copyright to all three books. A key component of the series is the artwork of Ulkatcho artist Ronald Cahoose, who created the covers for the books as well as illustrations of activities throughout the pages to accompany the text and stories told by the Elders.

More needs to be said about the eulachon grease that was such an integral part of Indigenous life. Grease was produced in a centuries-old process in which tonnes of smelt-like eulachon were netted in the mouths of glacier-fed rivers in early spring. It is said the temperature of the water was a big factor in determining when the fish would enter the rivers to spawn.

Through an elaborate process of rotting the fish for a week or more, then slowly cooking the decomposed fish all day in vats of boiling water, the grease was extracted and then processed further to preserve it. Traditionally the grease was stored in bentwood boxes or gut sacks and was a cherished food staple throughout the year. What wasn't consumed locally was traded to nations who were unable to produce the grease themselves.

Stanley King, Stanley Snow and Thomas Tallio with a herring seine of eulachons in 1997. By the 1970s this method of fishing had replaced the use of traditional long, conical nets made from nettle fibres. Sage Birchwater photo

In 1935 three men pry the conical net into their dugout spoon canoe while fishing eulachon in the Bella Coola River. Cliff Kopas photo courtesy Leslie Kopas

The Nuxalk caught eulachon or *sputc* using thirty-metre-long conical nets woven from stinging nettle fibres. The nets were set in the fast-moving water near the mouth of the river and held in place by stakes driven into the riverbed. The wide end of the net was held open facing upstream with the small end trailing downstream with the current.

Great schools of eulachon would enter the river on the high tide. Then as the tide ebbed, the fish would get washed into the nets by the current. The nets filled up with several tonnes of fish at a time and were emptied into long, narrow dugout spoon canoes by untying the narrow end and dumping the fish into the boats. It was a laborious undertaking that required the efforts of three or four men working together. The canoe had to be held steady in the current while section after section of the long net was pried into the canoe using a bent hemlock stick so the fish could be worked through the net and out the small open end. Someone had to be steadily bailing as the dugout filled with fish. Often there were only a few centimetres of freeboard to spare when the canoe was brought to shore. As they were unloaded, some of the large males were separated for drying in the smokehouse or for eating fresh, but the bulk of the catch was taken to large containers beside the river called stink boxes, lined with cedar boughs, where the fish could age sufficiently. Once the rotted fish were deemed ready for grease making, they would be scooped out of the stink boxes and taken to cooking boxes for processing.

"EVERYBODY'S GREASE HAS ITS OWN TASTE"

As told by Nuxalk Elder Andy Siwallace in Ulkatcho Stories of the Grease Trail *(Ulkatcho First Nation, 1993)*

"Each family had its own way to make grease. Some people like to stir the fish constantly all day while they are cooking. I just like to stir them once in a while, very gently.

"Some people let the eulachon rot a long time; others don't let them rot long enough. It all depends on the person making it. If the fish haven't rotted enough, the grease won't come out of them. Once they start smelling 'pretty ripe,' they are ready for cooking.

"The cooking box is filled with water and a fire is lit underneath it to get the water boiling. A long time ago, before we had metal cooking boxes, hot rocks were used to boil the water in bentwood containers. Then the ripe eulachon are scooped from the stink boxes and put into the boiling water. You've got to keep watching it. As the water begins to boil a bit, you stir the eulachon toward the place where it is boiling. If it boils too much, you add a little cold water to cool it down a bit.

"The grease begins to collect on the surface as soon as the eulachon are put into the boiling water. Once the fish have cooked long enough and most of the grease has come to the surface, the whole batch is mashed up with a paddle made with chicken wire. The flesh of the fish is broken up and cold water is added. This helps bring out even more grease. At this stage the grease making is very sensitive.

"If the mashed-up fish are cooked too hot, the grease will disappear right before your eyes. They say the grease has gone back to the fish when this happens. You never get it back. The whole batch of grease can get lost this way. It happens to a lot of people.

"One time it started to happen to me and Silas King [a member of the Nuxalk Nation]. We were making grease together and our grease started to disappear. As an experiment we tried adding more rotted fish from the stink box. After we added three more tubs of eulachon, the grease started to come back. We saved most of it. [Nuxalk Elder] Fred Schooner said we were the first ones he ever heard of who got their grease back.

"While it is still cooking, the grease is ladled from the surface and put into smaller containers so it can be cooked a second time to remove the impurities. If you don't recook your grease, inside of a month it will get so rancid it's not even funny.

"I like to use the traditional method of hot rocks to recook the grease. They say mine is the slow way but I prefer it. Hot rocks change the whole taste of the grease. You can smell the difference right away. I get my rocks from the river and build a special fire to heat them up. When they are red hot, we wash them in a tub of hot water, then put them into the pots of grease. You don't put much grease in a pail when you recook. That way only two or three rocks are needed to get it boiling just right. When the boiling grease reaches the right sound—the right tune—then I know it's done.

"One cooking box full of eulachon can produce thirty gallons of grease. One family might get between fifty and sixty gallons of grease in a season. They are long days too. We go for a week getting up at four in the morning and going until eight or nine at night.

"One time we were visiting friends in Fort Rupert near Alert Bay on northern Vancouver Island, and they served some grease with our supper. After I tasted it I talked to my wife in our Nuxalk language. Our hosts wanted to know what we were talking about. I said we were trying to decide whose grease that was. We said it tasted like our neighbour's grease in Bella Coola. Our friends told us we were right, but they sure were surprised. Not only did we know the grease came from Bella Coola, but we knew who made it. Our friends wondered how we knew. It's not hard to tell, I told them. Everybody's grease has its own taste."

Nuxalk Elders Andy and Lillian Siwallace, Grace and Art Hans, Gert and Harvey Mack, Obie and Shirley Mack, Simmy Mack and Wilfred Tallio welcomed a group of Ulkatcho youths and Elders to their family grease-making camp along the Bella Coola River in the spring of 1991. It was mid-April, and several stink boxes of eulachon had been ripening for over a week and were ready for making grease.

Ulkatcho youths Michael Sill and Clarence Cahoose got right into shovelling rotted eulachon from the stink boxes into buckets and hauling them to the cooking boxes. Dave Dorsey Jr. helped stir the fish mash as it gently cooked away. As the grease rose to the surface, it was ladled into smaller pots where Grace and Art Hans oversaw the recooking process. They used hot rocks to bring the golden-coloured liquid to a boil, skimming off impurities as they bubbled to the surface.

Nearby over a campfire, Ulkatcho Elder Helen Squinas steadily cooked panful after panful of fresh bannock in the newly rendered grease to feed the hungry workers. *Tl'enaghe* is the Dakelh word for eulachon grease.

For many of the Ulkatcho youths, this was their first time witnessing a grease-making operation. Learning by doing is a tried-and-true way to gain understanding.

"And don't bother trying washing your clothes after making grease," Simmy Mack warned his guests. "Just throw them away once you are done."

Few people had any idea that 1997 would be the last year the *sputc* would come to the Bella Coola River in sufficient numbers to make grease. I headed down to the valley from the Chilcotin at the end of March with my companion Sandi Giovanelli and her seven-year-old adopted Tŝilhqot'in daughter, Angela. When we got to Bella Coola we gave Andy Siwallace a call. He told us the eulachon hadn't come into the river yet, and we were quite disappointed. But early the next morning, on April 1, Andy called to let us know the fish had arrived overnight. We were elated.

Andy brought us down to the river, where a skiff tied next to the shore was full of eulachon. He said we could help ourselves.

"Nuxalk custom is to give the first catch of eulachon away to the community," he said.

Andy held a bag as Angela filled it with *sputc*. Then he asked us back to his house, where he and his wife, Lillian, showed us their regalia of button blankets, headdresses, drums and rattles. That's when Lillian told us how Andy's mother, Margaret Siwallace, had led the cultural revival of the Nuxalk language and culture forty years earlier (see "Andy and Lillian Siwallace" chapter). They were on the verge of being lost forever, she said.

THE TANYEZ TEZDLI GATHERING

Ulkatcho Chief Jimmy Stillas hosted a gathering at Tanyez Tezdli in August 1987 to celebrate the grease trail and all that it represented. He wanted to spark a revival of ancient customs. It had been thirty years since a gathering had been held at this special place along the grease trail on the back side of the Rainbow Mountains from Highway 20. What was significant about Tanyez Tezdli for the Ulkatcho First Nation was that it was the only place completely within their territory where salmon could be harvested.

Historically several families had smokehouses at Tanyez Tezdli to preserve their year's supply of fish. But by 1987 these post-and-beam structures had rotted and collapsed.

One important goal of the 1987 gathering was to establish Indigenous sovereignty along the Nuxalk-Dakelh Grease Trail. "We were afraid of losing the culture of our trail," Chief Stillas said. "Tanyez Tezdli was used as a gathering place as far back as I remember."

A year or two earlier, Quesnel probation officer Sandy Brunton had organized a trail ride for Nazko and Lhoosk'uz youths to follow the grease trail all the way to the Bella Coola Valley. Then in 1987 he organized a similar, week-long wagon trip and trail ride to bring Nazko and Lhoosk'uz youths to Tanyez Tezdli. This time there were hundreds of people at the gathering site to welcome them.

The Sill and Cahoose families pose for a photograph at the 1987 Tanyez Tezdli gathering. Left to right: Minnie Sill, Nadine Charleyboy Sill, Beverly Charleyboy, Susan Hance, Beryl Sill, Carmen Hance, Emily Sill, Byron Parker, Gurney Cahoose and Herb Sill. Sage Birchwater photo

Chief Stillas wanted to document the event, so he invited the media to cover it. The *Vancouver Sun* sent reporter Jeff Lee and photographer Ian Lindsay. I wedged into a de Havilland Beaver float plane at Nimpo Lake to represent the local media. As we approached Tanyez Tezdli we could see more than a hundred horses staked in the meadow below. Many Ulkatcho members had ridden to the site by saddle horse from Anahim Lake and Salmon River country farther down the Dean River, where several families have ranches. On a rise of ground above the meadow was a bustling campground of tents and campfires.

A primary focus of the gathering was to catch the spawning spring salmon collecting in big pools in Takia Creek, which drained Tanyez Tezdli. The fishing holes were below a waterfall a kilometre or two downstream from the camp, which prevented the big chinooks from migrating farther upstream. In the camp, Elders were showing youth how to fashion spear hooks out of broken hay-fork tines or spikes salvaged from derelict smokehouses. Once they were bent and sharpened, they were affixed to long poles with the gaff facing forward like a spearhead. The detachable point was connected to the shaft of the spear by a length of stout cord. The device was designed to have the hook dislodge from the pole once it struck the fish, leaving the fish dangling from the pole by the suspended cord. It was an ingenious design improvised and perfected over millennia.

Those attending the 1987 Tanyez Tezdli gathering pose for a group photograph. Left to right, standing: Gabe Sill, Pamela Holte Garner, John Roorda, Timothy Cahoose, Sarah Sill, Tilda Sill holding Kandi Sill, Peter Alexis, Larry Cahoose, Minnie Alexis, Larry Moody, Susan Hance, Mack Squinas, Gurney Cahoose, Jimmy Stillas, Minnie Sill, Wilfred Cassam and John Cahoose. Sitting: Martin Toney, Nick Sill, Agness Cahoose, James Toney, Lillian Siwallace, Joe Cahoose, Eliza Saunders, Clayton Mack, Cheryl Siwallace and Carman Hance. Sage Birchwater photo

The Tanyez Tezdli gathering was like a classroom where the Elders passed their first-hand knowledge on to the younger generations. This was Chief Jimmy Stillas's plan. This sacred tradition of continuity and transference of learning was what the residential schools had disrupted by forcibly removing children from their communities and families. Chief Stillas described the gathering as a place where people ate together, socialized and communicated with one another. Games were played, stories were told, and songs were sung.

I was struck by the wildness of the place. Grizzly bear tracks were embedded in the trail that followed the river to the prolific fishing sites. Someone said the grizzlies always walked in the same footprints as they made their way through the thick underbrush, and these tracks were worn down into small pockets. It was spine-chilling to be in that place. Our sheer numbers of two hundred souls occupying the site provided some reassurance the large omnivores would give us a wide berth, but their presence could be felt everywhere.

After a day's wait, the convoy of trail riders from Nazko and Lhoosk'uz arrived. They had travelled in four wagons for a week from Nazko to the

Andy Cahoose tries spearing fish by horseback. Sage Birchwater photo

Alexie Cahoose, Andy Cahoose and others stand poised with fishing spears in Takia Creek. Sage Birchwater photo

Left: Susan Hance and Bev Charleyboy wash a big chinook salmon caught in a gill-net in Takia Creek. Right: Gabe Sill stands with his spear while his brother Beryl scans Takia Creek for fish. Sage Birchwater photos

Russell Cahoose, Wayne Sill and Leo Stillas put together a gaffing spear in camp. Sage Birchwater photo

Andrew Cahoose holds his two-month-old granddaughter June Cahoose Lulua. Sage Birchwater photo

Ulkatcho Elder Salhkus stands by her smokehouse at Tanyez Tezdli in 1934. The roof of the smokehouse is covered with slabs of spruce bark. The old woman's tent is pitched under the smokehouse for shelter. Cliff Kopas photo courtesy Leslie Kopas

Dean River. There they parked their wagons and continued on by saddle horse and pack horse over the more rugged and narrow horse trail.

Legendary Nuxalk grizzly bear guide and hunter Clayton Mack was there to greet the riders. He was somewhat diminished compared with when I had met him fourteen years earlier at the grease camps along the Bella Coola River. He had suffered a stroke that confined him to a wheelchair and was living in the Bella Coola hospital. But he had recovered sufficiently to venture into the wild places like Kimsquit and Tanyez Tezdli, assisted by Jimmy Stillas's half-brother Larry Moody. Clayton was an avid storyteller, determined to pass on his culture, knowledge and wisdom to emerging generations. His family was resigned to Clayton's unique role.

"He belongs to the community now," his wife later told me.

I was awed by the ease with which multiple generations of Ulkatcho families camped in the wild. Pat Sill, flanked by sons Beryl and Michael, shoed his horses using a campfire as a forge and a flat, bevelled rock as an anvil. He pounded the heated horseshoes with a hammer until they fit snugly on his horses' hooves. His wife, Minnie Sill, and her mother, Mary Joe Cahoose, sliced freshly caught salmon to feed the hungry throng and to hang in a makeshift smokehouse to dry. Mary Joe's husband, Joe Cahoose, sat resolutely nearby beneath a tree, contemplating the scene.

For the Ulkatcho, Lhoosk'uz, Nazko and Nuxalk Peoples, this is what the Nuxalk-Dakelh Grease Trail was all about. It was the main corridor through the heartland of their country linking their communities together. But big changes were in the wind.

Henry Jack points out a mass grave he witnessed at Tanyez Tezdli when he was a kid. Sage Birchwater photo

By the 1950s the federal government had established an Indian residential school at Nagwuntl'oo (Dalkehl for Anahim Lake) and children were removed from their homes. The federal government assimilation policies did not support building houses on remote Ulkatcho ancestral home areas, but insisted on moving families to a central location in Anahim Lake. Ulkatcho citizens were taken from their self-sufficient livelihoods and placed on a social welfare system. The Grease Trail was still utilized to hunt, trap and travel down to Bella Coola, but as time progressed it was used less and less as the road from Williams Lake to Anahim Lake was extended to Bella Coola.

Another big impact on the Southern Dakelh way of life in the early 1950s was the construction of the Kenney Dam on the Nechako River. The provincial government gave Alcan (Aluminum Company of Canada) permission to create the gigantic Nechako Reservoir to generate hydroelectric power at Kemano for the company's aluminum smelter in Kitimat, without consulting the Indigenous people affected. Travel routes between Ulkatcho and Cheslatta were cut off, and family members who had intermarried from both communities were separated. In addition, huge swaths of hunting, trapping and hay meadows were lost to the flood.

HENRY JACK AND THE TANYEZ TEZDLI SMOKEHOUSE PROJECT

Henry Jack grew up along the Grease Trail with his grandfather Baptiste Stillas at Squinas Lake, just west of the Dean River Crossing. As a boy, Henry would go trapping with his grandfather.

"Me and old Stillas used to go around all the time and go trapping," he told me. "One time we followed the Dean River almost to Salmon House Falls at the mouth of Takia Creek. It was four days down the river, then up the mountain to Tanyez Tezdli. We come out by Squinas Lake. When we got to the Dean River I wondered how we were going to get across. My grandpa cut some dry logs and took some dry sticks and tied them all together with a rope. Old Stillas behind and me up front, we paddled across the river. My grandfather used to camp all winter trapping.

Henry Jack supervises the construction of the smaller of two smokehouses at Tanyez Tezdli in 1992. Ulkatcho youth and Elders worked together to build it. Sage Birchwater photo

The larger of the two new smokehouses is being utilized as a camp shelter and kitchen. Sage Birchwater photo

Dave Dorsey Jr. leads a pack horse on the Grease Trail heading to Tanyes Tezdli. Sage Birchwater photo

"At Tanyez Tezdli several families had smokehouses there. We dried salmon in there and camped in them. There were three smokehouses at Tanyez Tezdli and another down below the falls by the fishing hole. That way if you caught some big spring salmon you didn't have to pack them all the way back."[54]

He said the Stillas, Jack and Johnny families owned one of the smokehouses, the Alexis family owned another, and one belonged to the Cahoose family.

"Tŝilhqot'in and Nuxalk people would come to the Tanyez Tezdli gatherings as well," Henry said. "The Sulin family, the Joe Granbush family and people from Nemiah went down to Tanyez Tezdli too."

Sitting on a big split rock at the Tanyez Tezdli campground, Henry told a story of people dying at that place.

"So many people died there was no one left to bury them. Their bodies were piled up in the crack between the rocks. I remember seeing human remains there as a kid. The hair still on a skull."

Ulkatcho Elders believe the deaths were the result of the 1918 Spanish flu pandemic that occurred ten years before Henry was born.

In the summer of 1992 the Ulkatcho community hired Henry to oversee the construction of two brand new smokehouses at Tanyez Tezdli. A summer youth employment program, Challenge 92, provided the workforce for the project.

Smokehouses are simple structures, essentially a roof mounted on a post-and-beam log frame. They provided an ideal place to pitch a tent throughout the year. Historically slabs of spruce bark were used as roofing material. For Henry's project, shakes were split from lodgepole pine and nailed on the lattice of pole rafters for the roof. Marvin Paul, a Lhoosk'uz man married into the Ulkatcho community, spearheaded the shake production, splitting them with a froe, while Elders Peter Cahoose, Andy and Mack Cahoose and others trimmed the shakes to the proper thickness. It was a group effort with an army of young people packing the shakes to the building site and nailing them in place.

---

54   Henry Jack, quoted in *Ulkatcho Stories of the Grease Trail* (Anahim Lake, BC: Ulkatcho First Nation, 1993), 24.

Ulkatcho Elders Andy Cahoose and Mac Squinas share their knowledge of traditional plants with linguist Leslie Saxon and ethnobotanists Michele Kay and Richard Hebda. Sage Birchwater photo

While the smokehouses were being constructed, an ethobotany research team headed by Nancy Turner and Richard Hebda from the University of Victoria and the Royal BC Museum interviewed Elders about the traditional use of plants for food and medicine. Michele Kay, a grad student under Nancy Turner's tutelage, recorded the interviews with Elders Maddie Jack, Eliza Leon, Mac Squinas, Andy Cahoose and his brother Andrew Cahoose, Monica Sill, Wilfred Cassam, Lucy Dagg Dester Sulin, Helen Squinas, Henry Jack, Mary Jack, Peter Cahoose, Annie Cahoose, Mary Joe Cahoose, Eustine Squinas, Frank Sill, Marvin Paul, Kelly Moffat, P.L. West and others.

Four years later, in 1996, the information given by the Elders was published in the book *Ulkatcho Food and Medicine Plants* (see "The Ulkatcho Book Series" sidebar, p. 140).

In the fall of 1992, Henry Jack provided more details about the Nuxalk-Dakelh Grease Trail on a pack-horse trip with outfitter David Dorsey Jr. and Ulkatcho culture and curriculum leader Leona Toney. I was part of this expedition, recording Henry's stories for *Ulkatcho Stories of the Grease Trail*. Henry had stories about every twist of the trail from the top of the Bella Coola Hill to the Blackwater. Traversing the open subalpine of the Rainbow Mountains, he described his family's numerous trips along the grease trail to Bella Coola.

"After haying time, all the Ulkatcho people would leave home and head to Bella Coola. The Ulkatcho Johnny family, Captain Harry Alexis, Charlie West, Captain Casmiel Alexis Sr., they would all go down to

Ulkatcho Elder Mary Joe Cahoose took a leading role in the Tanyez Tezdli gathering, cutting up fish and mentoring younger members of her family. Sage Birchwater photo

Ulkatcho Elder Joe Cahoose spent his whole life along the Grease Trail, trapping, hunting and packing. Sage Birchwater photo

dig spuds. Our family would go too, but first we would hunt caribou in the Rainbow Mountains and make lots of dried meat for winter. My dad would take all that dried meat to our house at Squinas Lake where we lived along the grease trail. Then we'd go down to Bella Coola too and dig spuds by hand and pick apples, pears and cherries. There were apple orchards and potato fields all the way from Canoe Crossing Bridge to Hagensborg. Day after day we'd be digging spuds, forking up each side of the row. One guy came behind and put the spuds in a sack. Another guy came behind and tied up all the sacks and put them together in piles, two or three sacks in one place. If you filled up three hundred-pound sacks, they'd give you one sack free," Henry said.

"On the way to Bella Coola everybody in the family had their own horse to ride.

"In the fall, coming back, we were all on foot. All the saddle horses were packing apples, carrots and spuds. We all walked back. Going up the steep mountain trail following Burnt Bridge Creek, the kids would hang on to the horses' tails. Crossing the little creeks, we'd jump on behind the pack, then get off on the other side."[55]

At Mackenzie Pass, the high point along the grease trail through the Rainbow Mountains, there's some gravel scree at the base of a volcanic cone. If you look carefully, you can see tiny sparkles coming from the gravel. Closer examination reveals small, rounded pebbles of obsidian, known as *bes* to the Ulkatcho. It was a treasured commodity during pre-contact times. With the introduction of steel and metal tools by European and Russian traders, obsidian diminished in importance. Traditionally it was used for making knife blades, arrowheads and spearheads. The old-timers knew about the quarries where big chunks of this volcanic glass could be found. On the mountaintop, only marble-sized pieces sit in the gravel, but it is a hint of the rich potential that exists in this country. *Bes* from Anahim Lake was traded as far away as the prairies beyond the Rocky Mountains.

The winding trail down the switchback slope of Mackenzie Pass takes you to picturesque Mackenzie Valley. If you look on official government maps, everything in this vicinity has Alexander Mackenzie's brand on it.

In the scenic bowl at the base of the pass sits a small log cabin nestled in the trees, called Rainbow Cabin. Henry Jack referred to it as the Tommy Walker Cabin. It was Tommy Walker who built it in the 1930s using the sharply tapered logs that grow there in the alpine. The trees are short in height, wide at the butt and skinny at the top, but can be fashioned into a comfortable refuge in the wilderness by a skilled craftsperson.

Tommy Walker came to Canada from England in 1929, the year Henry Jack was born, and was instrumental in lobbying the government

---

55   Henry Jack, quoted in *Ulkatcho Stories of the Grease Trail*, 28.

Ulkatcho Chief Jimmy Stillas and his uncle, Henry Jack, grew up together along the Nuxalk-Dakelh Grease Trail, where they learned the ways of the country from their grandfather, Baptiste Stillas. Sage Birchwater photo

to designate Tweedsmuir Provincial Park as a protected area. A three-hour horse ride from Tommy Walker Cabin takes you to Tanyez Tezdli. Henry said this was his family's trapping area. Continuing down the grease trail, Henry pointed out the homestead where he grew up with his father and mother, Jamos and Emma Jack, and siblings John, Patrick, Minnie and Benny, at Squinas Lake. Abandoned for more than forty years, the shake roof was falling in. A big twisty pine full of large branches growing right beside the grease trail was a tree Henry had climbed as a kid.

Henry said his family also had a house at Ulkatcho Village, about thirty kilometres farther east along the grease trail.

"Every Sunday we went to Ulkatcho Village to go to the store. Sunday was the only day the storekeeper was home."

Not far past the Jamos Jack homestead, Henry pointed out his grandfather Baptiste Stillas's old cabin next to the trail. The roof, covered with sawn lumber planks, was still intact. Henry got off his horse, sat on the old bench beside the front door and rolled himself a smoke.

"Them old people had trails all over the place," he said. "People lived all over. Every five or six miles there would be another lake and a family would live there."

Lillian and Andy Siwallace in their traditional Nuxalk regalia. Photo courtesy the Siwallace family

ANDY AND LILLIAN SIWALLACE

Andy and Lillian Siwallace were true ambassadors of Nuxalk traditions and culture in the Bella Coola Valley. Always generous, they willingly shared their stories and demonstrated their culture openly. But the rich accumulation of language, art, dancing, drumming and song was something they had to work hard to restore after decades of cultural repression. Lillian credited Andy's mother, Margaret Siwallace, for leading the cultural resurgence in the Nuxalk community.

MARGARET SIWALLACE

Margaret was born in Kimsquit at the mouth of the Dean River in 1908. As a young girl she attended potlatches at Kimsquit in her grandfather Charlie Saunders's longhouse. She was one of only four children in the village when her father, Joe Saunders, took her to the Crosby Girls' Home in Lax Kw'alaams (Port Simpson) north of Prince Rupert in 1916. She was nearly eight years old when her dad dropped her off at the school for Indigenous girls run by Methodist missionaries, and she felt so out of place because she didn't know a word of English.

A week later another Nuxalk girl, Lina Clellaman, arrived at the school, but Margaret and Lina were forbidden to speak their Nuxalk language. The other children were Tsimshian, and the same rule applied to them. No one was allowed to speak her own Indigenous language. Little by little Margaret learned to speak English from the other girls she played with.

After two winters at the school, Margaret came down with whooping cough in the spring of 1918 and was confined to the hospital in Port Simpson for three months. Then in September her father brought her home to Bella Coola just as the flu pandemic was starting to devastate the community. Margaret's mother and granny were dead by that time, so she stayed with her father's sister in Bella Coola. As fortune would have it, neither Joe Saunders nor Margaret's future husband's father ever caught the flu, and it was their job to bury the dead who succumbed from the disease.

Nuxalk women celebrate VE Day in 1945 dressed in their traditional regalia. Seated, left to right: Annie Johnson, Anna Schooner, Helen Schooner, Flossie Webber and Amanda Siwallace. Standing: Agnes Edgar, Emily Schooner, Mabel Moody, Gertrude Schooner, Marjorie Tallio, Annie Tallio and Margaret Siwallace. Cliff Kopas photo courtesy Leslie Kopas

"Sometimes there were two deaths a day. Sometimes there was just one," Margaret told CBC's Imbert Orchard in a 1960 interview.[56]

Much has been said about the role the Catholic Church played in the demise of Indigenous cultures in Canada, but the United Church, then known as the Methodist Church, was equally culpable. The churches took their marching orders from the federal government in Ottawa.

"We were told by the [Methodist] missionaries to forget about Indian ways," Margaret told Orchard. "Forget your language and things like that."

Lillian Siwallace said Margaret dedicated her life to bringing back the Nuxalk language and culture. Basket weaving, dances, songs, mask carving and the potlatch were in danger of being lost.

"She brought back the button blanket," Lillian told me. "There weren't many left when she got everyone sewing the blankets again."

Button blankets are an important part of Nuxalk regalia worn at

---

56   Margaret Siwallace, interview by Imbert Orchard, 1960, tape number IH-BC.59, transcript disc 178, CBC Imbert Orchard Collection, University of Regina, https:// ourspace.uregina.ca/bitstream/handle/10294/894/IH-BC.59.pdf?sequence=1&isAllowed=y.

special cultural celebrations like pot-latches and community feasts or dances. Historically the woollen Hudson's Bay blankets were transformed into button blankets by west coast Indigenous Peoples using dentalium and abalone shells. These shells and later buttons or beads were sewn in the shape of crest designs belonging to the wearer and owner of the blanket.

When the potlatch was banned in 1885, this name-giving ceremony, key to passing on cultural identity from one generation to the next, was forced underground. Masks, blankets, rattles, whistles and other cultural artwork were seized by the government. Some members of the community who had converted to Christianity burned their Nuxalk artwork and regalia. Much of what wasn't destroyed found its way into museums around the world. Just a small number of button blankets and masks

Margaret Siwallace received many accolades for sharing Nuxalk culture and traditions. Grant Thomas Edwards photo used with the permission of the Siwallace family

were kept hidden from authorities. Meanwhile, children sent to residential schools were fed a diet of indoctrination and shame toward their culture that took many years to undo.

In 1985 Margaret was given her doctor of letters by the University of British Columbia in recognition of her devotion to intercultural understanding and documentation of Nuxalk culture. The citation for her *honoris causa* degree reads in part,

"She was an excellent translator, moving easily between English, Chinook, and her own native Nuxalk. An intercultural woman of great personal and scholarly integrity, Siwallace was the principal source for many papers and theses in fields that ranged from ethnobotany to linguistics, history to nutrition, and ethnomedicine to pharmacology. A true scholar and scientist in her own right, she fought for First Nations rights, working for her own community as well as for good relations amongst others. Siwallace mediated and unravelled many knotty problems in politics, law, customs, science and more general scholarship. … [She] has always been generous of herself, freely sharing with others the qualities and wealth of her mind and heart, her knowledge, her sympathy and her insight."

Lillian Siwallace with her grand-daughter Cheryl Wilson and great-granddaughter Emilie Margurite Graham during the de-commissioning ceremony for Emmanuel United Church. The totem doorway of the House of Noomst can be seen in the background behind them. Sage Birchwater photo

I met Lillian Siwallace for the first time in July 1987 at the Ulkatcho gathering at Tanyez Tezdli. This was a unique and special event in an isolated corner of Ulkatcho Traditional Territory on the Nuxalk-Dakelh Grease Trail. Traditionally Southern Dakelh, Tŝilhqot'in and Nuxalk people got together there in late July and August to catch salmon, trade and celebrate together. But for many years the gathering hadn't happened. There were several reasons for this, but a key influence was the building of the Bella Coola Highway through the Coast Mountains in 1953 that rendered the grease trail a less popular travel route.

Ulkatcho Chief Jimmy Stillas spearheaded the gathering in an attempt to revive this important coming together of people. He saw it as an opportunity for the Elders to pass on their knowledge of the land and way of life to the younger generations who had never experienced them before.

Lillian was one of several Nuxalk Elders invited to the gathering from Bella Coola. She was accompanied by her sister Grace Hans, cousin Eliza Saunders, uncle Clayton Mack, granddaughters Robin and Cheryl, and Larry Moody, Jimmy Stillas's half-brother.

Later that fall Lillian paid me a visit in Tatlayoko Valley, where she accompanied her husband on a deer-hunting expedition into the valley. While Andy was stalking his prey, Lillian sat at our kitchen table visiting. She was particularly intrigued by the bumper crop of soapberries (soopollalies) we had canned that year. Somewhere along the way we struck a deal to trade canned soapberries for canned salmon.

Soapberries (*Shepherdia canadensis*), known as *nawus* to the Dakelh, *sxusem* (shooshem) to the Secwépemc, *nuŵish* to the Tŝilhqot'in and *nux̱ski* to the Nuxalk, is the ingredient for making "Indian ice cream." Indigenous people across British Columbia enjoy this delicacy, but soapberries don't grow on the coast. As a result, they became a valuable trade item between the interior and coastal peoples. Members of the Tŝilhqot'in and Dakelh communities would dry the succulent red berries into berry cakes of fruit leather, which they traded with the Nuxalk for eulachon grease and other products from the sea.

That's probably how my relationship with the Siwallace family really began. We gave Lillian a case of canned soapberries, and she promised to give us some jars of canned fish when we next came to Bella Coola.

Over the years we had many meaningful exchanges with Andy and Lillian, who openly shared their knowledge of Nuxalk ways, culture and stories of the past. In 1998 they invited us to a great family potlatch jointly hosted by the Siwallace, Hans and Mack families. Andy was Hereditary Chief of the Siwallace clan, Lillian's brother Obie Mack was Chief of the Mack family, and Chief Art Hans represented the Hans family.

A few years earlier they had schooled us on the intricacies of making eulachon grease when we brought a group of Ulkatcho youth and Elders from Anahim Lake to Bella Coola. Andy and Lillian, Grace and Art Hans and Obie Mack hosted us at their family grease-making camp.

Andy's Story: A Lifetime of Relearning His Culture

Andy Siwallace was nine years old when he was sent away to residential school in Fort Rupert, near Port Alice on northern Vancouver Island. The year was 1934, and when he returned to Bella Coola six years later, he didn't know a word of his Nuxalk language. He had done well in his studies but, approaching his sixteenth birthday, he was too old to remain in school, so his mother, Margaret, sent him out to go fishing with his great-grandfather Peter Nelson.

The old man didn't know much English and Andy couldn't speak Nuxalk, so they communicated the best they could using sign language. Eventually Andy became so frustrated with the communication difficulties that he began speaking to his great-grandfather in English.

"I talked to him in English for a long time," he told me.

Not to be outdone, the old man responded by speaking to Andy in Chinook and Nuxalk. Andy was dumbfounded.

"I thought I was so smart because I could speak English. Now all of a sudden I realized I wasn't all that smart. I could see that my great-grandfather knew a lot too. From that day forward I decided to learn my language."

Andy Siwallace mending his net in his backyard in Bella Coola. Siwallace photo collection

That's when Andy's cultural education really began. For the next two and a half years he went from Elder to Elder, learning as much as he could about the four dialects that make up the Nuxalk language.

"The old people had so much fun with me," he said. "I made so many mistakes at first, they laughed at me. But that just made me more determined."

His great-grandfather's words and actions had removed a huge barrier in Andy's mind that had prevented him from wanting to learn about his culture. Something inside his brain fundamentally shifted. Not only was he interested in his language, but he wanted to learn the songs, dances and mythology of his people as well. He set about learning the old dances and discovered how they were a vital way for the old stories to be preserved and passed on to others.

Finally Andy got the chance to prove his worth. At a big community meeting he was asked to translate a letter from the Native Brotherhood, a First Nations rights organization, for the Elders. He stood before them and translated directly from the written English, and the old people were impressed. "They really liked it and they were really proud of it," he said.

That was an important turning point in Andy's life. From then on he was determined to represent his culture.

A masked dancer performs during a youth-run potlatch at Acwsalcta School in Bella Coola. Sage Birchwater photo

LILLIAN'S STORY OF CULTURAL REVIVAL

"We lost our culture over the years. The church came and changed our lives."

Lillian said the decades from the 1920s to the early 1960s were the dark days of Nuxalk culture. "We were prosecuted for potlatching, and in Bella Coola most of the old masks were hidden away in an attic," she told me.

Then in the early 1960s a group of Nuxalk women decided it was time to bring the culture back. "We had a meeting and decided that if the men weren't going to do it, then we would," she said. "The older ladies still knew how to dance."

Lillian said an older woman told her she should be a dancer.

"'I watched you as you were growing up,' she told me. She must have seen me jitterbugging." The older woman said that if Lillian could jitterbug, she could learn traditional Nuxalk dances.

By the early 1960s there were only one or two button blankets left in Bella Coola. What was left of the masks was brought out, and the cultural revival was underway. Lillian made her first button blanket from an old trench coat that she took apart and flattened out.

"In the '60s we didn't have access to the number of buttons we have today, so we cut them off old clothes. Of course they were all different shapes and sizes."

The first dances were held as fundraisers.

"We charged people to come in and watch us dance," Lillian said. "By 1970 we made enough money to send twenty dancers to Victoria. Then in 1972 we went out again."

Lillian's personal crest was the whale, so a whale was outlined in buttons on her blanket. Andy's personal crest was an eagle, and he had a button design of an eagle sewn on his blanket.

"It didn't take the men long to get in step with the cultural revival once the women started dancing," Lillian said.

Along with their button blankets, the Siwallaces' regalia included button vests, carved headdresses, rattles and a drum. All of these items were worn or used in ceremonial celebrations, which started happening more and more frequently.

"Years ago the church accused us of worshipping our masks and traditions," Andy said. "Actually we were play-acting our old stories from the beginning of time. One dance depicts how the thunderbird came to the aid of four men who were lost in the mountains."

The Nuxalk word for potlatch is *Lhlm*, which translates as "standing up for yourself." When the potlatches were outlawed, the Nuxalk still had them but called them "feasts."

"No merchandize was given away," Lillian said. "But an old guy would put on a feast and put out food, apples, crackers and money.

They always had a huge pot of stew and everybody brought along a little pot to take some of the stew home with them."

"The more a certain Chief put feasts up, the more he gained in status," Andy explained. "When I was a kid, they only brought out the masks at very special occasions, and they had to be very secretive about it. They took people back into the woods to learn to dance, and we didn't even know who the dancers were."

Along with the resurgence of making button blankets, many Nuxalk members started carving masks, rattles, spoons and even silver jewellery. In the mid-1980s a program was started in the Nuxalk-run Acwsalcta School to educate young people in the whole spectrum of Nuxalk art, language and culture. Lillian taught the Nuxalk language there.

"There's still a ways to go to bring the culture back," Andy reflected. "And keeping it strong is still a challenge."

Lillian said each generation of young people has its own likes and dislikes and preferences.

"One group of kids may be strongly motivated to embrace their culture, while the next group may want nothing to do with it."

There's a coffee mug and collector's plate in my cupboard that I've treasured for more than thirty years. They were gifts from Andy and Lillian Siwallace. Engraved on both is a likeness of the old Emmanuel United Church that once stood proud on the Nuxalk side of Burke Avenue in the Bella Coola townsite. The cup and plate were part of a fundraising campaign to replace the old church.

Lillian and Andy Siwallace display a fundraising souvenir plate used by the congregation of Emmanuel United Church to generate money to replace the old church. Sage Birchwater photo

Thanks to Goodwill Ambassador Darren Edgar, who conducted tours of special places in the Bella Coola Valley, I got introduced to the old church a number of times. What impressed me most was the building's acoustics. You could literally hear a pin drop resonating off its cedarwood-panelled walls. But the iconic structure was showing its age. Many of the stained glass windows were cracked, and it was feared the bell tower was so structurally unsound that it was dangerous to ring the bell.

I was shocked when Andy told me one day that the long-range plan was to tear down the old church and replace it with a new one. From my perspective as an outsider, the sixty-five-year-old structure was a heritage building worth preserving. But Andy and Lillian saw it differently. The old church was drafty and cold, especially in winter when the east wind blew down the valley from the high Chilcotin Plateau. The farther you go down the valley toward the mouth of the river, the greater the intensity and velocity of this outflow wind, known by the Nuxalk as the *sps*. The Bella Coola townsite receives the full brunt of its force.

"It's too cold to meet in the main part of the church with the east wind," Lillian explained. "So we have to hold the services in the back."

The church's unique, amazing and colourful history was one of Andy's favourite stories to tell. "It's the only church to ever be towed across the river," he would start out.

I was spellbound. Andy said he was away in residential school at Fort Rupert in the spring of 1938 when the bell tower and windows were dismantled from the 17-by-8.5-metre (56-by-28-foot) structure and the church was jacked up, put on log skids and towed across the Bella Coola River.

The timing for this intrusion into the river was vital. Salmon and eulachon were essential for the well-being of the Nuxalk People, so they had to wait until the eulachon had finished spawning and had to be finished before the first runs of spring salmon entered the river. They also had to take advantage of the low water levels before the spring freshets and melting snow brought the river into flood.

Lillian was six years old and hadn't been sent away to residential school yet, so she witnessed the whole thing.

Since the 1880s the Nuxalk had had two villages at the mouth of the Bella Coola River. On the south side was Q'umk'uts, the traditional village with its ancient longhouses. On the north side was a modern village with European-style lumber-frame houses, a community hall and the brand new Emmanuel United Church.

A brief history might help explain.

Before European contact, the Indigenous population of the Nuxalk Nation was around three thousand people, inhabiting up to twenty villages along the fjords from Kimsquit to South Bentinck Arm and from Kwatna in Burke Channel up the Bella Coola River sixty-five kilometres to Stuie. After the smallpox epidemic of 1862, the population suffered a catastrophic collapse with a death toll estimated at more than 70 percent of the people. This forced the abandonment of outlying Nuxalk villages and the congregation of people at Q'umk'uts at the mouth of the Bella Coola River.

Five years later, in 1867, the Hudson's Bay Company opened a trading post in Bella Coola next to Q'umk'uts. Years later, Hudson's Bay employee

The old Methodist Church, built in 1905 in the Nuxalk Village on the north side of the Bella Coola River. It was torn down in 1935, and building materials were used in the construction of Emmanuel United Church. Photo courtesy B.C. Central Coast Archives

John Clayton took over the store and the company property. The company had also had a trading post in Bella Bella on the outer coast since 1843. A Methodist church was located in Bella Bella as well, and this was the closest bastion of Christianity to Bella Coola. Though missionaries would occasionally show up in Bella Coola, the Nuxalk population remained steadfast in their own spiritual beliefs and traditions.

In 1882 something changed. Nuxalk Chief Tom Henry, who was responsible for taking care of the masked song and dance ceremonies, had a religious conversion to Christianity. According to his grandson Bill Tallio, speaking at the 2001 decommissioning ceremony for Emmanuel United Church, Tom put down his masks, headdress and cloak and invited the Christian missionary William Henry Pierce from Bella Bella to begin ministering to his people. The late Ed Moody, former Nuxalk Chief, said in the 2006 documentary *From Bella Coola to Berlin* that Tom burned two wooden boxes of his regalia in front of the Methodist minister.[57]

Tom's conversion caused quite a schism in the Nuxalk community. Half the people followed Tom to the north side of the Bella Coola River, where they built a new village at the mouth of the Necleetsconnay River, and the other half remained at Q'umk'uts on the south side of the river and kept to their old ways. Church services for Tom Henry's followers were held in a longhouse until 1905, when a Methodist church was constructed to replace the longhouse as a place of worship.

Despite the decimation of their population from smallpox and other introduced diseases, the Nuxalk still outnumbered the settlers in Bella Coola until the first boatload of eighty-four Norwegian colonists arrived on October 30, 1894. This was followed by two more boatloads of Norwegians the following year. The bulk of the colonists settled farther up the Bella Coola Valley at Hagensborg, but in 1895 a white settlement was built next to the Nuxalk village on the north side of the river.

57 *From Bella Coola to Berlin*, directed by Barbara Hager (Victoria, BC: Bella Coola to Berlin Productions, 2006), DVD.

There were several reasons for this. The north side of the river was sunnier and had more fertile ground for growing crops like potatoes. There was also better access to the port facilities thanks to a kilometre-and-a-half-long pier constructed to provide access to the government wharf located at the base of a cliff in the deep water on the north side of North Bentinck Arm.

The two communities on the north side of the river had one drawback: they were susceptible to the periodic devastating flooding of the Necleetsconnay River. The white community on the north side was the first one to blink. After putting up with thirty years of intermittent flooding, they finally had enough when the Necleetsconnay washed out the whole town in 1924. Premier Duff Pattullo declared it an emergency. The next year the white population relocated to the south side of the river, where a townsite was laid out on the old Hudson's Bay property once owned by John Clayton.

The Nuxalk community on the north side remained steadfast, confident they could withstand the elements. In 1934 they started building a new church to replace the old Methodist church that was too small for its growing population. By that time the Methodists had merged with the Presbyterians and other faiths to form the United Church of Canada. So the new church completed in 1935 was named Emmanuel United Church. To forge a link between the past and the present, wood from the old church was used in building the new structure. Then came the flood of 1936. That was the last straw. Not only did it take out most of the houses, but it washed out the roads and waterworks infrastructure and took out the only bridge across the river that linked the north side to Q'umk'uts and the new Bella Coola townsite on the south side. The Nuxalk residents on the north side finally abandoned their village site and joined the rest of the community south of the river.

The Emmanuel United Church being towed across the Bella Coola River in April 1938. An engine fan briefly gives the bulldozer driver a shower before the fan belt is disconnected. Cliff Kopas photo courtesy Leslie Kopas

The Nuxalk brass band played "Onward Christian Soldiers" inside the church sanctuary as it was being towed across the river. Cliff Kopas photo courtesy Leslie Kopas

One of the buildings not ravaged by the flood was the brand new Emmanuel United Church, so plans were made to move it across the river. On April 21, 1938, a small bulldozer hooked onto the skids placed under the church to tow it across the Bella Coola River. But the church wouldn't budge. So they hooked up a second small Caterpillar and tried again. Same result. Two Cats still couldn't move it.

Then, as Andy Siwallace liked to put it, "some smart Indian went into the church and checked, and sure enough the church's chimney was still attached to the ground." With this problem rectified, they managed to coax the church four hundred metres the first day. The next day they launched into the river with both bulldozers straining on the tow cables. The engine fan on one bulldozer gave its driver a brief shower until the fan belt was disconnected.

"I remember my grandmother and a whole bunch of ladies standing on the riverbank crying," remembered Lillian. "They were afraid the church might sink."

In a fanfare of celebration, the Nuxalk brass band set up inside the church to play "Onward, Christian Soldiers" as it was floated across the river. Andy said they played the whole way across.

"My dad, Stephen Siwallace, was in that brass band. They got wet up to their waists but they kept on playing."

Once across the river, they set the church up on Burke Avenue, where it remained for sixty-three years.

In one day, the eighteen-month-old Emmanuel United Church was relocated to the old village site of Q'umk'uts south of the river. Cliff Kopas photo courtesy Leslie Kopas

Emmanuel United Church stood close to the site of the old village of Q'umk'uts. By 1938 the Nuxalk community had mostly reconciled the divergent belief systems of Christianity and traditional Nuxalk spirituality. Over the years the church became a community repository for spiritual memory. Weddings, funerals, banquets, Christmas concerts and blessings of all types were held there. The church served as a bastion of religious life.

The church sat for more than six decades on the original skid logs used to drag it across the river. No foundation was ever built under the sanctuary, and by 2001 the floor was rotting and the roof was sagging. Metal rods were installed across the sanctuary as a stopgap measure to keep the walls from splaying out and collapsing.

United Church minister Betty Sangster lived in the manse across the street from the church. "Every morning I would look over to see if the church was still standing," she said at the church's decommissioning ceremony in 2001. "Four years ago we were told the building should be condemned."

Despite the church's decrepit condition, the sanctuary retained its magnificent acoustics. Sangster said she sang in church choirs all over Canada, but few facilities equalled the resonant qualities the wood-panelled walls provided for Emmanuel United Church. As with an old musical instrument, perhaps, the sound quality just got better and better with age.

Back in the 1930s when the church was first built, there were no sound systems to amplify voices and music, so the acoustics of the church were key. Sangster figured it was the shape of the sanctuary.

Darren Edgar at the Thorsen Creek petroglyphs, which he showed visitors when he took them to the valley. Barry Brower photo

Andy Siwallace said members of the early congregation made their own vigorous sound using trombones and trumpets.

"My father played any kind of instrument, but the brass band sort of came to an end when the old people died."

For ten years the congregation worked to raise money for a new church. Lillian Siwallace said five women spearheaded the fundraising drive: Hazel Hans, Louisa Schooner, Veronica Andy, Mercy Snow and Annie Schooner. The activities included bingos, raffles and telethons. Mercy Snow said the most money they ever made was at funball.

"We sold fries, hamburgers and hotdogs."

Bella Coola's goodwill ambassador, Darren Edgar, was a devoted Emmanuel United Church member. He had a tough go of it as a child when he got hit by a car while riding his bicycle. He suffered a serious brain injury and was prone to epileptic seizures the rest of his life. Despite these challenges, he managed to turn his disability into something positive. He credited Barbara Pedersen, a long-time Bella Coola resident, for mentoring him.

Darren's brain injury reduced the social filters that govern most people, so he was unabashed when it came to walking up to strangers newly arrived in town and offering to guide them to various points of interest in the Bella Coola Valley. One of these special places was the Nuxalk petroglyphs up Thorsen Creek. Another was the House of Noomst Elders' longhouse, where you entered the building through a door in the face of a carved figure on a totem pole. A third was Emmanuel United Church, which stood next door to the House of Noomst.

When you went on a tour with Darren, you felt transported to another time and place. It was as if his altered state of consciousness were contagious. At the petroglyphs, for instance, he would sit quietly and let the majesty of the place speak to you. In the House of Noomst the artistry and the smells of cedar and smoke connected you intimately to the beauty and mystery of Nuxalk culture. Entering Emmanuel United Church with Darren, you immediately felt the sanctity of the place and the reverence Darren felt for this house of worship.

For sixty-three years Emmanuel United Church stood on the corner of Burke Avenue and Cliff Street in Bella Coola, providing a spiritual refuge for the Nuxalk community. Then on July 8, 2001, the congregation held a special decommissioning ceremony for the building. It was time to let the old church go. The paint was peeling, the moss-covered shingles were tired, and the bell tower was too rotten to dare ringing the bell. I was there as a journalist covering the event for the local newspapers.

Minister Betty Sangster led the ceremony, joined by regional United Church minister Paul Davis from Williams Lake. A dozen Nuxalk Chiefs and Elders, including Andy and Lillian Siwallace, sat in a place of honour at the front of the sanctuary to assist with the program. Boxes of tissue were placed on the pews as the church leaders anticipated an emotional farewell. The scripture chosen for the thought of the day was Ecclesiastes 3:1–8, words familiar to the '60s generation: "For everything there is a season, and a time for every matter under heaven …"

The story of the church's history was told: how it was built by volunteers from the Nuxalk community in the early 1930s in the village on the north side of the river, and how parts of the old church built in 1905 were used in its construction to offer continuity and to honour the Elders who were part of that early church. And it was told how the church was jacked up and dragged to its present location on the south side of the river after the devastating flood of 1936 washed out the village. Then

Emmanuel United Church Minister Betty Sangster goes over the ceremony script with former Nuxalk elected chief councillor Archie Pootlass. Sage Birchwater photo

The congregation of Emmanuel United Church gives a final blessing by circling the old facility during the decommissioning ceremony. Sage Birchwater photo

various members of the congregation shared their personal stories of the church that contained a wealth of special memories over six decades.

Former elected Nuxalk Chief Councillor Archie Pootlass stood up and said he wanted to talk about the healing that still needed to take place before the old church was taken down and a new facility was built in its place.

"We heard previous speakers talk about the sadness and remorse in losing this facility, and about the celebration for the new facility to come, but I want to talk about the healing that needs to happen as we move forward."

He said his personal quest for healing involved forgiveness.

"Many of us are survivors of residential school syndrome. Personally I was sent to Port Alberni for four years. Though the federal government was financially responsible for that institution, it was the United Church that ran it. Personally I have a lot of painful memories from attending residential school. Now it's time for me to forgive the United Church for managing and administering that facility."

Both Ministers Sangster and Davis embraced Archie after he finished speaking, accepting his forgiveness on behalf of the United Church of Canada.

"It is difficult for men to apologize and forgive," Davis said. "It is with humbleness and gratitude that I accept your forgiveness. It was the brokenness of my ancestors that inflicted brokenness on your ancestors."

Various Elders took turns speaking. Hazel Hans remembered times before the church was built. "When I came in and saw all the people here tonight, it reminded me of when the church was across the river, and how important the church was in the old days."

Lorna George said a lot of prayers had been answered in the church.

"My grandpa used to pray every morning in this church. Very early too. At five in the morning."

Bert Snow, with his guitar in hand, acknowledged his sadness.

"This is the last time I'll be singing in this old church. That's how it is with life. Something always ends and something always begins. Now that the end is here, so is the beginning."

The ceremony concluded with children leading the congregation outside, carrying the Christ candle and forming a big circle around the church. Minister Davis reflected on the mingling of joy and sorrow.

"This is a sacred place and a sacred space," he said. "I sense the people who built the church in the walls, ceiling and floor which hold the memories of the people married and Elders buried here."

Church Elders performed one last rite eleven days later, on July 19, 2001. They lit a ceremonial fire and burned some food and pieces of wood taken from the old church as a show of devotion to those who built the church. Speaking in Nuxalk, Andy Siwallace named the old people from the past.

"This is an act of giving the church back to those people," he explained.

Then, as if to lend some supernatural pronouncement to the occasion, the church bell that had been silent for years, and too tired to ring during the decommissioning ceremony eleven days earlier, rang once.

"No one pulled the rope; no one was around," Andy said later. "It just rang. That was really something."

Two days later, on July 21, a small crowd gathered as contractor Mark Nelson positioned his excavator to start the demolition. The whole previous week, many Nuxalk members had helped themselves to wood and materials stripped from the church. This included the stained glass windows, doors and seasoned lumber. Lastly the bell was carefully extricated from the bell tower.

Darren Edgar sat on a couch perfectly positioned on Cliff Street so he, his mother, Millie, and friends Pearl

Mark Nelson's excavator starts to topple the old church. Sage Birchwater photo

The old bell, which wouldn't ring during the decommissioning ceremony, mysteriously rang once eleven days later during a ceremonial fire honouring the Elders. Sage Birchwater photo

Snow and Christine Dawson had front-row seats. As the teeth of Mark Nelson's excavator bit into the bell tower and started to topple the structure, Darren let out a cry of anguish and started sobbing uncontrollably. It was a combination of extreme joy and gut-wrenching sorrow for him. I wheeled my camera around and got a memorable shot of the four of them sitting together. Darren brightened up, and they all shared a laugh.

That would be my last photograph of Darren Edgar, Bella Coola's goodwill ambassador. Over the fall and winter, the new Emmanuel United Church was constructed on the footprint of the old church, but this time with a sound cement foundation. As the new building neared completion, plans were made to hold the first service on Easter Sunday.

Sadly Darren never made it.

He had been planning to be a part of this inaugural ceremony and had expectations to incorporate the new church into the rounds of his successful but low-key tourism venture. But tragedy struck in the wee hours of that Easter Sunday morning on March 31, 2002. Darren was alone, walking at first light along the deeply ditched roadway in the Bella Coola townsite, when he suffered a grand mal seizure. The convulsions threw him violently into the water-filled ditch, and he drowned. His lifeless body was discovered later that morning.

Darren Edgar, Pearl Snow, Millie Edgar and Christine Dawson watch the church demolition with a mixture of joy and sorrow. Sage Birchwater photo

Easter is about the resurrection of Christ, and this symbolism isn't lost with Darren Edgar. He was a man of faith and devotion with a strong commitment to good works. He left this world on a day sacred to his beliefs.

I was standing with Andy Siwallace on the front porch of the brand new church as people were coming out the doors after the service. Perhaps it was the official grand opening of the facility, I don't re-

Nuxalk Elders Andy Siwallace, Lillian Siwallace, Archie Pootlass, Bill Tallio, Hazel Hans and Obie Mack lead the decommissioning ceremony at the front of the sanctuary in Emmanuel United Church. Sage Birchwater photo

member. Andy and Lillian were respected Elders in Emmanuel United Church and strong Christians. They were also pillars in the Nuxalk cultural community, teaching the language and leading potlatch and dance ceremonies.

Suddenly Andy turned around and pointed to the rounded hill half-way up the mountainside above the church.

"That's the hill that saved our people from the flood," he said matter-of-factly.

I had a hard time hiding my astonishment. I was witnessing a curious blend of mythology: Christianity on one hand and the ancient Nuxalk cosmology on the other, all spoken in a single narrative. I marvelled how Andy and his fellow Nuxalk congregation members managed to straddle both worlds and belief systems so effortlessly. It felt like he was devout and faithful to both. He was also colour-blind when it came to sharing his stories with a white guy like me.

Andy's son Peter Siwallace helped put it into perspective.

"Dad was always guarded about sharing our Nuxalk history with his kids," he told me. "He would tell an outsider like you, but with his children he was quite closed about some things. I think he was still affected by the brainwashing from residential school where he was told his language and his culture weren't worth knowing. Dad was severely punished at residential school for speaking his language or talking about his culture, so I think for our protection he didn't want to teach us. It was hard for him to share stories of the past with me. It's like he was saying to me,

'You're better off not knowing that stuff.' He shared some stories with you he never told us about."

Realizing the depth of the trauma his dad had suffered at residential school was a big turning point for Peter.

"It was a big eye-opener for me once I realized what my dad went through," he told me. "I basically forgave my dad. I hadn't realized how badly he was brainwashed. Later in life he changed. At potlatches he proudly and openly started sharing all aspects of Nuxalk culture, traditions and stories."

Peter said his grandmother Dora Mack also told the story of the mountain that saved his people. "My grandma said when the big flood came, the good people made it to the mountain. Then as the water rose, the hill rose too. Our Nuxalk stories go back to the beginning of time when there was no light. Just like the old stories in the Bible."

ACKNOWLEDGEMENTS

As a freelance writer and a resident of the Cariboo Chilcotin Coast for nearly half a century, I compiled boxfuls of stories about the people and history of the region. Much of this material was published in various books, magazines and newspapers over the years. Upon revisiting some of these stories, Caitlin Press publisher Vici Johnstone suggested shaking out some of these accounts from days gone by as the foundation for a new book, *Talking to the Story Keepers*, in which we would expand on the original works by reaching out to the community to fill in the gaps to bring forward the voices of those telling the stories.

So, that's how it began.

The process was intriguing, but also a source of anxiety. I worried that families may not want these stories of their loved ones revisited. However, as I began to reach out to communities and individuals, the response was soon overwhelming. A wealth of new information flooded in, and the stories took on a life of their own, adding to the narrative like the wind filling the sails of a great ship. As family members shared their stories, the narrative took on the guise of a living document filled with new information.

My writing over the decades has always included a strong Indigenous perspective. I was hired by the Ulkatcho Nation more than thirty years ago to interview their Elders and assist with documenting their culture and history for generations yet to come. Today, as Indigenous societies have greater capacity to tell these stories on a broader scale themselves, my role has shifted. In *Talking to the Story Keepers*, I've attempted to balance the voices of Indigenous and non-Indigenous speakers as equal partners in presenting an historical perspective of the Cariboo Chilcotin Coast.

There are a few people and organizations whose input was invaluable in the unfolding of these stories. I would like to give a special thanks to: Chris Wycotte, Roseanna McGregor, Dinah Belleau, Kim Kaytor, Rob Diether, Joyce Charleyboy, James Lulua Sr., Dinah Lulua, Roger William, Lorraine Weir, Diana French, the late Bev Butler, Rita Lulua Meldrum, Bruce Baptiste, Joanne Gregg, Judy Gregg, Garry Gregg, Jack

Gregg, Mack Dester, Elaine Dester, Elliott Dester, Dereck Sill, Liz Anderson, Janie Jack, Bill Poser, Chief Lynda Price and the Ulkatcho Elders Council, Gertie Capoose, Maureen Sill, James Jack, Hárvey Sulin, Laurie Vaughan, Bella Leon, Mabelene Leon, David Dorsey Jr., Joyce Dorsey, Ed Ober, Halle Flygare, Linda Flygare, Stan Boyd, Leona Toney, Susan Turner, Gideon Schuetze, Marilyn Siwallace, Peter Siwallace and Carl Siwallace.

Also thanks to Alex Lulua, Fred Brigham, Junah Birchwater, Diane Toop, the family of Veera Bonner, Rene Morton, Paul Kopas, Leslie Kopas, the Siwallace family, Nancy Turner, Kent Apa'tsti Danielson and Harriet Kuhnlein for their help tracking down photographs and giving permission to use their images and original artwork.

I want to dedicate this book to Caterina Geuer, whose companionship and love continues to nourish and inspire me, and to the story keepers of the Cariboo Chilcotin Coast and their families who made this book possible.

Opposite: Addie Saunders (left) and Mary Jane McEwan share a laugh at Jimmy Stillas's funeral in November 1990. Addie was the wife of Mary Jane's biological father, Joe Saunders. Sage Birchwater photo

Photo Gallery

Thomas Squinas (left) and Joe Sill at Nimpo Lake. Joe and Thomas were insepara-
ble companions in the last years of their lives. Their signature move was to drive very
slowly around Anahim Lake in Thomas's truck. Here they are on the shore of Nimpo
Lake. Sage Birchwater photo

Opposite: The men are engaged in a game of lahal. Left to right are Benny Lulua,
Bernard William (looking at the camera), Ubill Hunlin and Tommy Jack. Sage Birchwater photo

Peter Cahoose helps his sister Eustine Squinas cut up salmon at their fish camp at Canoe Crossing in the Bella Coola Valley. Sage Birchwater photo

Elders' feast celebrating the grand opening of the Jimmy Stillas Learning Centre in Anahim Lake in 1990. Thomas Squinas (left) and Peter Alexis share some stories while eating their meal. Sage Birchwater photo

Connie King was a professional hockey player who moved to Anahim Lake to become a rancher. When he lost an eye after getting attacked by a grizzly bear, his fraternity of former pro hockey players came to his aid until he could get back on his feet and resume ranching. He was one tough old guy. Sage Birchwater photo

Minnie Sill cuts up a salmon at Tanyez Tezdli during the 1987 gathering hosted by Chief Jimmy Stillas to reinvigorate Ulkatcho culture and traditions along the Nux-alk-Dakelh Grease Trail. Sage Birchwater photo

Mary Jane McEwan (left) and Monica Sill share a story at Monica's birthday celebration in the early 1990s. Sage Birchwater photo

Henry Jack relaxing with a smoke at a gathering at Tanyez Tezdli in the early 1990s. Sage Birchwater photo

Susan Sulin Cahoose at a gathering at Tanyez Tezdli in the early 1990s. Susan was a leader and revered matriarch of the Sulin/Cahoose clan, always leading by example. Sage Birchwater photo

Timothy Sill was the third eldest son of Aggie Bouchie Sill and Thomas Sill of Ana-him Lake. Together with his brothers Frank, Joe, Pat, Eugene, Edward and Eagle Lake Henry, Timothy could trace his ancestry to Stuie in the Bella Coola Valley. Sage Birchwater photo

Pat Sill drives his team and wagon in Anahim Lake. With him are his wife, Minnie, and mother-in-law, Mary Joe Cahoose. Sage Birchwater photo

Art Stobie, Vivian Cahoose and Theresa Holte, along with Vivian's grandsons Owen Cahoose and Stewart King celebrate the grand opening of the Jimmy Stillas Learning Centre in the early 1990s. Sage Birchwater photo

Stó:lō educator Michael James brought his Indigenous traditional games program to Tanyez Tezdli in the early 1990s. His big ball was a favourite with the Ulkatcho youth. Sage Birchwater photo

Brothers Sammy (left) and Georgie Leon display some of their musical genius during the inaugural Elders Feast event at the Jimmy Stillas Learning Centre. Sage Birchwater photo

Andy Siwallace encourages Angela Giovanelli to fill a bag with sputc (eulachon) after explaining how the first catch of the fish goes to the community. Sage Birchwater photo

Ulkatcho Elders (top left) Wilfred Cassam (top right) Eliza Leon, (bottom right) Josephine Capoose Robson always generously shared their knowledge and expertise. Sage Birchwater photo

(Bottom left) A painting of Ralph Edwards by Ralph O. Easterbrook. Photo courtesy Diane Toop, Station House Gallery, Williams Lake

Nuxalk Elders Orden and Lucy Mack were honoured guests at an event in Anahim Lake hosted by the Ulkatcho community. Orden's brother Clayton Mack was married to Doll Capoose of Ulkatcho. Seated beside them is Japheth Izatt-Sill. Sage Birchwater photo

Boyce Squinas (left) and Anthony Peterson ride horseback in Anahim Lake. Sage Birchwater photo

INDEX

ABOUT THE AUTHOR

PHOTO CRAIG SMITH

Sage Birchwater is the author of *Chilcotin Chronicles* (Caitlin Press, 2017), *Chiwid* (New Star Books) and *Williams Lake: Gateway to the Cariboo Chilcotin*. He was a staff writer for the *Williams Lake Tribune* until 2009, and he was the editor of *Gumption & Grit: Extraordinary Women of the Cariboo Chilcotin* (Caitlin Press, 2009). Sage lives in Williams Lake, BC, and continues to write about the Chilcotin.